LONGSHORE
SOLDIERS

LONGSHORE SOLDIERS

Homefront ★ England ★ Normandy ★ Antwerp

LIFE IN A WORLD WAR II PORT BATTALION

ANDREW J. BROZYNA

APIDAE PRESS
Longmont, Colorado

Apidae Press
www.ApidaePress.com

Copyright © 2010 Andrew J. Brozyna

ISBN: 978-0-9827811-0-4 paperback
ISBN: 978-0-9827811-1-1 hardcover

For a hardcover library edition visit www.ApidaePress.com

Visit www.519thPortBn.com for additional articles and photographs.

Designed by Andrew J. Brozyna, AJB Design, Inc., www.ajbdesign.com
Typeset in Miller, DIN 1451, and Trade Gothic.

Printed in the United States of America.

Dedicated to Grandpa Corty and all the port battalion men who served in World War II

CONTENTS

PREFACE

In the summer of 2006 I came down with the flu. It was one of those illnesses making it too unpleasant to sleep. I took the opportunity offered by those late nights to watch the Band of Brothers series on DVD. In between segments the camera focused on actual veterans speaking about their experiences. One man talked of his grandson's questions about the war. I immediately thought about my own grandfather and the fact that I had not spoken to him about his service. Shortly after, I began calling my grandfather with an idea to record a few of his Army stories.

As our weekly talks progressed I read books to better understand his service. A friend of mine, a retired Army officer, suggested I contact the National Archives for information about my grandfather's 519th Port Battalion. The reading spurred new questions.

I discovered two other veterans from his unit. During the Vietnam conflict my grandfather's unit was reactivated as the 519th Transportation Battalion. Soldiers from this more recent war created an association website. Here I found WWII veterans Dave Weaver and Bruce Kramlich. I spoke to them and they referred me to other veterans. In 2009 I created a blog to chronicle my research. More port company veterans and family members found the site and contacted me. They shared their stories and photographs.

What began as a short collection of my grandfather's anecdotes became a thorough unit history. At the beginning of my research I was surprised to find there was so little published about the work of the Army port companies. I am pleased that my small book will contribute to the scholarship of World War II, but the process itself has been valuable on a personal level. My frequent interviews brought me closer to my grandfather and introduced me to ten men with a shared past.

ACKNOWLEDGEMENTS

My thanks go to: all the veterans and veterans' family members who shared their time, stories, and photographs; my wife, Kelly, for all her suport; my mother, Patricia, for her hours reading through microfilm at the Schenectady County Public Library; Cindy Seacord at the Efner City History Center, Schenectady, NY; Dina Linn at the US Army Transportation Museum; Tracy Dungan for his time and his knowledge of the V-2 rocket; Charles Oellig at the Pennsylvania National Guard Museum at Fort Indiantown Gap; Robert Morgan for his knowledge of WWII Wales; Raf Boesmans for his research at the Felixarchief Antwerpen and his knowledge of WWII Belgium; and Erica Hill and Jenny Hunt for editing and proofreading the text.

IMAGE SOURCES

Photograph captions in this book include an abbreviation indicating the source of the image. All maps are by the author.

PERSONAL COLLECTION ABBREVIATIONS

Andrew J. Brozyna	(AJB)
Anya M. DeLaura	(AMD)
Tracy D. Dungan	(TDD)
Solomon Fein	(SF)
Terry Johnson	(TJ)
Bruce C. Kramlich	(BCK)
Peter Sloboda	(PS)
Israel Sugarman	(IS)
Dave H. Weaver	(DHW)
Gary Wanczak	(GW)

ORGANIZATION ABBREVIATIONS

Efner City History Center	(ECHC)
Naval Historical Foundation	(NHF)
Pennsylvania National Guard Military Museum, Fort Indiantown Gap, Annville, PA	(PANG)
U.S. Library of Congress	(LOC)
U.S. National Archives	(USNA)
U.S. Army Transportation Museum	(ATM)

Cortland Hopkins
before the war. (AJB)

Francis, Catherine, Vivian, and Edward Hopkins. (AJB)

1

SCHENECTADY

It all started on Sunday, December 7, 1941. A lanky twenty-seven-year-old, Cortland "Corty" Hopkins, stood in front of the bathroom sink shaving. Music was drifting in from the next room's radio. The program was interrupted to broadcast a startling announcement. Pearl Harbor had been bombed. "Jimmy, where's Pearl Harbor?" His brother didn't know either, but they learned that the Japanese had attacked Hawaii. To picture this easygoing man as angry would be difficult for anyone who knew him. Yet, all the Hopkins brothers were furious and eager to defend their country.[1]

On Monday morning Cortland headed off to his job at S. S. Kresge's Five and Dime.[2] He was head stock clerk at this small store on the corner of State and Jay streets in Schenectady, New York. Just before opening he asked his boss if he could take a break. The boss said, "Sure, go ahead," so Corty walked out the door intending to enlist in the Navy. The post office just a few blocks away housed a military enlistment office. He approached the Navy recruitment officer and was quickly met with rejection: "You've got varicose veins and not enough teeth." "But, I'm not going to bite them." Corty tried to argue. "I'm going to *shoot* them." The critical recruiter was not impressed with this skinny, seemingly unfit man standing in front of him. "He didn't even look at my legs. He just had to write something down on the paper. I guess 'varicose veins' was the easiest thing to write."

Waiting in line for his mail, a small-time gangster recognized Cortland. They had met several years previous when Corty worked as a bicycle courier. Cortland had met all sorts of colorful Schenectady characters while delivering packages for Western Union. The gangster came to Cortland's defense, challenging the officer's decision. This dubious character reference was less than helpful. Corty returned to work at the Five and Dime.[3]

The Japanese-made products in the Five and Dime immediately dropped in sales. No one wanted to buy trinkets made by the enemy. Kresge's business-savvy manager displayed a sign with the ceramic figurines and trinkets saying, "Defeat Japan! Sales Go To War Bonds." The stuff sold out instantly. Corty hoped that his boss was truly buying government bonds to support the war effort, but he wasn't so sure. On Wednesday the 10th, Nazi Germany and Fascist Italy declared war on the United States. Cortland again tried to enlist, this time with the Army. Failing to meet their fitness standards, he was rejected. Cortland's more robust brothers and most of his friends had successfully enlisted. Eldest brother James was sent to the Pacific in one of the Naval Construction Battalions (the "CBs" or "SeaBees"). Cortland's younger brother, Francis, also joined up, serving in the Pacific as a signalman aboard a Navy landing craft.[4] Youngest brother Eddie was too young to join up. After the war he would enlist in the Air Force, serving in occupied Japan. When asked what his young sister was doing during the war, Corty quipped, "Worrying."[5]

Unable to serve in the military, Corty felt rather useless. His parents, on the other hand, were greatly relieved. "I guess everybody was happy I didn't get in." Marge was happy too. Marjorie Bulow had been "going with" Corty for a number of years. She worked as a secretary at Schenectady General Electric plant. The two had met at church—St. George's Episcopal Church, located in the heart of the Stockade District of Schenectady. When Marge first caught his eye she was already in a relationship. There was even a marriage proposal, but she would not accept unless her boyfriend agreed to allow her parents to move in with them. Marjorie's father had suffered a stroke at an early age. Although he worked part-time, her parents needed financial assistance.

Kresge's Five and Dime, on the corner of State and Jay streets in Schenectady, New York, 1941. This photograph was probably taken from the top of Proctor's Theatre. (ECHC)

Her steady never did come to a decision on the matter. He was killed in a passenger airplane crash. A couple of years went by and Cortland asked her out. Marge's younger brother, Leonard, had shipped off with the Navy. She was especially glad that she need not worry about her boyfriend as well.[6]

One might wonder if practical concerns helped fuel his enthusiasm to enlist. At twenty-seven, Cortland was still living with his parents. He lacked the resources to support himself financially, let alone a wife and parents-in-law. The military offered a comparatively good salary, a chance to save money, and training potentially useful to civilian life. Adventure and independence from his parents could also have been attractions. If Cortland considered these, then it was only as ancillary advantages. Genuine patriotism was foremost in his mind. It was a feeling characteristic of his generation.

James Hopkins in the Pacific. (AJB)

2

AMERICAN LOCOMOTIVE COMPANY

In late 1942 Cortland would have an opportunity to contribute to the war effort. Schenectady's Alco plant put out a call for extra workers. Located at 30 Church Street, this was the headquarters for the American Locomotive Company. The factory was manufacturing for the US War Department, had moved to twenty-four hour production, and needed more workers. In Corty's words, "Alco sent for me." Alco men walked around town, hiring people on the spot. A 1993 article in the Schenectady *Daily Gazette* confirms this assertive approach to employment. Dominic Louis Bagnato, an Alco welder, recalled being sent out on the third shift to find new men and women for the workshops.[1] Corty was pleased to leave Kresge's to begin training as a welder.

A nearly 100-year-old institution, the well-established American Locomotive Company's Schenectady plant was ideally suited to meet the military's intensive production demands. During the course of the war 1,086 steam locomotives and 157 diesel-electric locomotives were built for the US War Department.[2] Its facilities were easily adaptable to the production of tanks and other weaponry. The factory managed to take on new military projects without interrupting its locomotive production. Before the attack on Pearl Harbor, Alco was already manufacturing tanks for the department. On November 23, 1940 Alco was awarded a contract to build the Army's M-3 medium tank, the "General Lee." The first completed tank rolled out less than five months later in April 1941.[3] Alco produced an improved version, the M-3A1, and

then in 1942 accepted a contract to build the M-4 Sherman.[4] This became the primary American tank used in the war. As production progressed company engineers improved their tank-building techniques. Many of Alco's innovations were so successful they were adopted by the nation's other tank manufacturers.[5]

Alco arc welders working on an M-4 tank in Schenectady, NY, 1943. (LOC)

There was great secrecy involved with this government work. Sabotage was a major concern. Windows were blacked out and workers were fingerprinted. Special badges were required for workers in departments producing weaponry.[6] Such precautions were common at all war production facilities, but in this case an honest-to-goodness secret weapon was involved—a mobile howitzer. The M-7 "Priest" was a 105mm artillery piece mounted onto the frame of the M-3 tank. Production began in April 1942. The US Army had initially ordered the M-7 for its own use, but sent the first completed models to the British Eighth Army in North Africa. The British debuted 1,000 of Alco's M-7s in the second Battle of El Alamein, Egypt (fought from October 23 to November 5, 1942).[7] The Brits nicknamed the M-7 the "Priest" because of the pulpit-shaped cab for the driver. The surprise weapon was instrumental in the German defeat at the battle and the overall Allied victory in North Africa.

Cortland's work was primarily spent on these M-7s, but he also welded tanks. "First I was working on locomotives, then they trans-

The M-7 "Priest." (LOC)

ferred me to over to the tank division. I welded the outside of the tank. The more experienced 1st class welders had the inside. I was 2nd class, so I had the outside."[8] With its high production capacity Alco was the country's second largest tank manufacturer. After Cortland left Alco in 1943 the company would go on to produce the M-36 tank destroyer.

THE "E" AWARD

Alco workers also constructed equipment for naval guns. In gratitude for the quality and high rate of manufacture, the Navy Department conferred their Navy "E" Award ("E" for excellence) on the plant November 18, 1941.[9] The Navy presented an award pennant to fly on the Alco grounds. Awardees were reviewed every six months. In May of 1942, the efficient Schenectady plant was permitted to continue flying their pennant for an additional six-month period. A white star was added to their banner as further confirmation of the excellent work.[10]

Alco's Schenectady plant received another "E" Award from the US War Department in August 1942, extending recognition to its Army projects. By this time the two branches of the military were giving a joint award to individual factories that "achieved outstanding performance on war production." The Army-Navy Production Award bestowed a pennant to the plant, and all employees were given sterling silver lapel pins. Only 5% of all American war manufacturing facilities would ever receive this honor. The award pennant was swallow-tailed, bordered with white trim, and featured a white capital letter "E" in a yellow wreath of oak and laurel leaves. The oak represented strength, while the laurel signified victory. The background was divided into red and blue halves. "ARMY" appeared in the red background and "NAVY" in the blue. The small pins also featured an "E" within a wreath of silver oak and laurel leaves. Horizontal swallow-tail wings flanked the pin's wreath. These wings featured five stripes—red at the top, white, blue, white, and red at the bottom.[11]

The president of Alco's Schenectady plant received notice of their Army-Navy Production Award on August 1, 1942.[12] On August 11, the *Schenectady Gazette* reported on the upcoming ceremony:

> Schenectadians soon will see the red and blue army-navy production award flag, to be bestowed upon the American Locomotive Co. for outstanding production achievement, flying from a staff atop a company building, keeping company with its navy "E" award.[13]

Across the country the receipt of an "E" Award was always an opportunity to express local pride and national patriotism. Award ceremonies at other plants typically included music from the local high school band or a Boy Scout troop to raise the flag. Several thousand

Alco workers gather in the Schenectady Yard to view the "E" Award presentation. (ECHC)

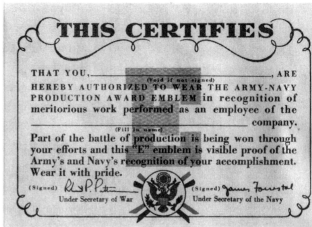

"E" Award certificate and pin.
Actual pin size is just under
15/16 in. or 14mm wide. (AJB)

Alco employees assembled outside to witness the award ceremony on August 27, 1942. The local paper estimated a crowd of 2,000, while Alco's wartime *Attack* newsletter set the count at more than 4,000. Whatever the exact number, it was a grand gathering. By the time Cortland set down his torch to join the onlookers, the lot was filled. At the back of the crowd, Cortland didn't have much of a view. He read about the details the next day. A platform was erected in front of the Alco laboratory building facing Erie Boulevard. In attendance were military representatives, local business and civic leaders of Schenectady, Albany, and New York City. The presentation began at 4 o'clock with local radio station WGY broadcasting.[14]

W. L. Lentz, manager of the Schenectady plant, acted as master of ceremonies. He opened the program by introducing a Miss Lucy Monroe, who sang the national anthem. Monroe was something of a celebrity in those days, a vocalist closely associated with patriotic public events. She had been featured in three separate weekly radio programs in the 1930s, starred in the 1940 New York World's Fair, conducted community sing-alongs to sell war bonds, sang for President Roosevelt, and would go on to sing for future Presidents Truman, Johnson, and Kennedy. New York Yankees fans would hear her sing the national anthem at every opening day and all the Yankees' World Series from 1945 to 1960.[15]

Maj. Gen. Charles T. Harris addressing the Alco crowd. (ECHC)

Mayor Mills Ten Eyck made opening remarks after the raising of the US flag. Captain J. S. Evans, the naval ordinance inspector for Schenectady factories, then presented the sterling lapel pins to Lentz and four representative workers. These pins were later distributed to all of Alco's 8,000 employees through department channels, complete with small personalized certificates. Lentz read out a congratulatory telegram sent by the Undersecretary of War. Commander of the Army's Aberdeen proving grounds, Major General Charles T. Harris, was the next to take the stage. He offered one corner of the "E" banner to Alco President Duncan Fraser. Nelson MacDonald, selected to represent the employees, received the other end. Harris spoke, praising Alco's tanks and other military production.[16] The general made no mention of the M-7, carefully preserving its secrecy. The *Schenectady Gazette* reported:

> "You have done splendidly," he told the workers, "but you've got to keep up the good work, you've got to better your present record; you've got to keep tanks rolling off the assembly line, more and even more. We've got to make sure, and you've got to help us make sure, that when the time comes for our big scale offensive against the axis we won't be lacking in material. You people are doing a wonderful job and are just as important to the army as the man up front who is doing the fighting."[17]

The award banner was raised to join the American flag. President Fraser gave an acceptance speech, commending his employees' increased output and encouraging their future efforts. The steelworkers' union was represented in this patriotic display by James Steele. His words offer a bit more passion than the more earnest speakers:

> "We of the C.I.O. again dedicate ourselves as free American workers to the task of staying on the production lines and

producing and producing and producing until Hitlerism, fascism, and every other vestige of slavery is wiped off this God-given earth of ours."[18]

A newly produced M-7 (foreground) and M-4 tanks at Alco in Schenectady, New York, 1943. (LOC)

Miss Monroe concluded the ceremony by leading the audience in a rendition of "America." The entire event took only thirty minutes, and the employees immediately returned to their work.[19]

M-7 DAY PARADE

Less than a year later, Alco would be honored again in a vastly more elaborate fashion. Alco's secret weapon, the M-7, had performed spectacularly well in North Africa. Its heavy cannon knocked out the enemy tanks and anti-tank artillery up to seven miles away. Faster than any German tank, the Priest's high mobility put it right where it was needed. The German tanks were devastated, while none of the M-7s were lost to the enemy. Five months after the victory at El Alamein representatives from the British and American armies came to Schenectady to express their gratitude. On April 10, 1943 Alco proudly announced the day's festivities in a full-page ad in the morning newspaper:

> Today's the day—the first birthday of the deadly weapon of war that helped turn the tide at El Alamein. And Schenectady has plenty of reason to celebrate.
>
> For the M-7 that helped leave 500 of Rommel's tanks blazing in the sands at El Alamein and drove him back through Tobruk and Bengazi and Tripoli to face his own Dunkerque—that "tank killer" was built right here in Schenectady, by Schenectady men and women. And it was kept a total secret from the enemy by every local citizen!
>
> That's why the bands will play today—why guns will salute—why American and British officers and other notables—including the workers who built the M-7—will take part in impressive ceremonies celebrating the event.
>
> That's why the world premier of the thrilling motion picture— Twentieth Century Fox's release of "Desert Victory"—will take place right here in town. For this picture is an actual record of one of the decisive battles in history, filmed right on the spot.
>
> Join the throngs who celebrate the important part Schenectady has played—and is playing—in clearing all roads to Berlin.
>
> This is M-7 Day—a day that is proudly Schenectady's own.[20]

The *Schenectady Gazette* described the M-7 Day program with a great sense of accomplishment. Praise was given to those who built the tank-killer and the citizens of Schenectady who maintained its secret. Completed M-7s had been in public view, driving from the plant to the Army proving grounds for testing. They were also visible when they were loaded onto train cars for shipment overseas. No pictures were taken, and no stories told until after Army authorization in January 1943.[21] There was a strong desire among all Americans to do their part for the war effort. Keeping quiet was a simple, yet important way to contribute. News of the German Army's defeat in Egypt and the British Army's public gratitude was met with satisfaction by the entire city. Local businesses filled the paper with congratulatory messages

M-7 Day parade progressing up Erie Blvd. Mayor Mills Ten Eyck appears at the bottom left corner. (ECHC)

to Alco. Townspeople lined the streets to watch the afternoon's events.

An M-4 parked at the Hotel Van Curler. April 10, 1943. (ECHC)

1:30 P.M. The celebration began with a parade of workers from the American Locomotive Company plant to the small park across from the Hotel Van Curler (currently Schenectady County Community College's Elston Hall).[22]

1:45 P.M. Special guests, workers, and citizens gathered at the park. Military music played, and there was a "firing of seven bombs in honor of the M-7's birthday."[23] Presumably, the "bombs" were blanks fired from the Alco tanks stationed around the park.

2:00 P.M. Colonel A. G. Cole, former commander of the 72nd Field Regiment of the British Eighth Army, described to the audience how the M-7s were used in the battle of El Alamein.[24] He shared the British victory with Alco's men and women:

> "I like to think that the Eighth and Schenectady armies were jointly responsible for the glory of El Alamein. American production cities are like armies themselves. You know them by their achievements."[25]

Major General Russell L. Maxwell then spoke. Maxwell had served as Chief of the US North African military mission and then as commander of the US forces in the Middle East. Maxwell commented on the quality of the work:

> With this success behind you there can be no doubt of your future and when the shooting stops you can look at the record with pride and return to the manufacture of locomotives with the satisfaction that comes only from the knowledge that the assigned job was well done.[26]

The general's sentiment predicted Cortland's own career. After the war he returned to Alco, then accepted a job at General Electric. He took pride in his work, welding until his retirement.

The ceremony continued as several other British and American military heads addressed the audience. Each speaker was welcomed to Schenectady and introduced by Mayor Mills Ten Eyck. In conclusion the mayor dedicated a time capsule containing objects associated with the M-7. Plant manager W. L. Lentz placed an Alco pennant in the

M-7 Day assembly outside Hotel Van Curler, Schenectady, NY. (ECHC)

concrete chest. Union leader James Steele and George Mabee, representatives of the workers, added tools. American Colonel Frank J. Atwood placed M-7 photographs in the capsule. Blueprints of M-7 parts were added, possibly by Alco President Fraser. Colonel Cole sealed the chest, and it was buried in the plaza with a commemorative stone placed above. The ceremony was broadcast over WGY radio.[27]

2:30 P.M. The mayor, military dignitaries, workers, tanks, and M-7s paraded up Erie Boulevard. Several bands played including a Scotch "Kiltie" band, an American Legion drum and bugle corps, and a marching band of war workers. The procession ended in front of the Erie Theater.[28]

3:15 P.M. Concluding the afternoon's events was a screening of the newly released British documentary "Desert Victory." Days earlier President Roosevelt had a private viewing courtesy of the commanding officer of the British Eighth Army film unit. The presentation at Schenectady's Erie Theater was the world premiere of the film. Saturday's showing was restricted to Alco employees, while the general public was admitted the next day. During the ceremony and parade Cortland's shift was busy working. They did, however, walk over for the premiere. He and the other workers appreciated seeing their M-7s in action. "Desert Victory" depicted the actual battle of El Alamein, including scenes from captured German film and dramatic footage taken by the British Royal Air Force and a corps of British Eighth Army photographers. Of the 26-man film unit, four men were killed, seven were wounded, and six were taken prisoner.[29]

3

IN THE ARMY NOW

Cortland was proud of his work at Alco, yet "I wasn't entirely happy. I wanted to enlist. I felt bad because all my friends were in, so I had to get in the service. I just *had* to. I'd get on a bus and people would look at me as if to say, 'Well, my son's in the service. Why isn't he?!'"[1]

Sometime in May or June of 1942 Cortland was excited to receive a draft notice. He brought the notice to work so he could inform his boss. "That was a big mistake. He got me deferred, because I was doing essential work." His boss was unwilling to lose a well-trained and skilled worker. He wrote a letter, deferring Corty's military service. Disappointed, Corty delivered the deferment letter. "One poor guy came out of the [recruitment] office crying, because they wouldn't reject him." To Cortland it seemed as though even guys who didn't want to go were getting called up. "This boxer I was walking down the street with, he was scared to death about going in the service. Oh, he was practically paralyzed! That poor guy, I felt sorry for him. I said, 'Sam, I'll tell you how you can beat the service.' He said, 'Tell me. I'm all ears, I'm all ears!' 'All you have to do is go down and get in one of the shipyards. They're looking for welders, and they're all deferred.' The next day comes, and he was gone to the docks. I did him a favor, and here I am trying to get in the service, and nobody wanted me."[2]

Cortland continued welding at the Alco plant. In late June or early July 1943 he came home to find he had received a second draft notice.

17

"I wanted to get in the service so bad I could taste it." This time he by-passed his boss and went straight to the recruiter's office. The military preferred not to take men away from war production jobs. Cortland was pleased to see the Army's records showed that he was still working as a store clerk—hardly essential work. He was careful not to correct that error. At last Cortland Hopkins was in the Army. Having signed the papers he went back smiling to work. He informed his boss, who offered to write up another deferment letter. "You're too late," he told him, "I'm already sworn in." His boss was "mad because I could have stayed out of the service."[3]

With two of their boys already in the Pacific, Corty's parents, Cortland Sr. and Catherine, were not at all pleased by the news. "They weren't too happy about it, but what can you do? All my friends were gone, and I wanted to go. I felt it was the thing to do." He did have some friends left in town. They took him out to dinner one night to wish him goodbye and good luck. "Some of them were 4-F and couldn't make it into the service. The thing that surprised me was that *I* was physically fit!"[4] Class 4-F was the Selective Service System's designation for those exempted from military service based on physical and mental standards. By this stage of the war the Army's physical requirements had been lowered, so Corty's skinny frame was not a hindrance as it had been two years earlier.

Marjorie kissed Corty goodbye, giving him an onyx ring to let the European girls know he was taken. Poor Marge was a naturally nervous woman. Worried about losing her sweetheart to German bullets or French women, she bristled at her mother's prediction that Corty would be bald by the

Marge & Corty. (AJB)

time he returned from overseas (Cortland's father was bald). Happily for Marge, Corty would survive the war and return with a full head of hair.

Cortland rode to Albany on July 9th, acting as "assistant leader" to a group of Schenectady County draftees. From Albany, the men boarded a train headed for the Army's Camp Upton in Suffolk County, New York. After three days Corty was sent by train to Indiantown Gap Military Reservation, Pennsylvania. Here, Corty joined young men from across the country for basic and advanced training.

FORT INDIANTOWN GAP MILITARY RESERVATION

Fort Indiantown Gap Military Reservation was one of the more important training camps during the war. A handy resource to this military center was published by the Bell Telephone Company of Pennsylvania. Presumably it was included in an orientation kit or was displayed in the fort's service centers. The introductory note from the manager reveals its mixed purpose—practical information for the new GIs and encouragement to call home:

> In this booklet you'll find some interesting information about Indiantown Gap, a list of the nearby Service Clubs, a map of the Reservation, several pages for notes, addresses and telephone numbers and a calendar. We hope you find it useful. Don't fail to visit our Service Men's Telephone Center.[5]

Although this was essentially a marketing piece for the local telephone company, the tiny guide offers a valuable description of the 1943 camp grounds. Named after the Delaware Indian villages that were once found in the area, Indiantown Gap was first used by the military when the Pennsylvania National Guard encamped there in 1931. The site was rather isolated, 14 miles north of Lebanon, 23 miles east of Harrisburg, and 46 miles west of Reading. In September 1940 the US Army took control of the camp. They rapidly replaced the National Guard tents with permanent buildings. The military reservation became a city unto itself, spreading over 26 square miles and organized into areas numbered 1 to 16. By April 1941 there were 1,138 structures, including headquarters buildings, fire stations, Post Exchange buildings, service clubs, guest houses, movie theaters, a sports arena, a hospital, a post office, a Red Cross office, chapels, band stands, a telegraph office, a telephone center, and a bus terminal.[6]

The Post Exchange or "PX" was a small store located at each of the camp's barracks areas. GIs could spend their pay on various luxuries such as candy, ice cream, soda, beer, and cigarettes. There were multiple service clubs at Indiantown Gap. The largest of these recreation centers was situated in the center of camp. Its cafeteria, library, auditorium, typewriters, and writing tables were available to military men day and evening. Family and friends were also admitted, but this was a rather empty gesture. Most troops were far from home, making visits impractical. Segregation was in full effect. Black troops used separate service clubs in the outlying areas 3 and 10. Areas 3, 4, 9, and 12 offered four large movie theaters operated by the US War Department. A 15-cent ticket admitted a soldier to a presentation of "the latest movie picture attractions" or the occasional USO show. Regimental or battalion bands gave concerts in each of the sixteen areas.[7]

The bus terminal was located in Area 3 near the service club. Most men used the bus for quick day-trips to Harrisburg, which featured its own USO clubs and service men's center.[8] A few times Cortland received a three-day pass, although getting home was not easy. "We had to parade every morning, so I couldn't leave until the afternoon. We had to take a bus to Harrisburg, then a train to New York City, and another train to Schenectady. By that time I was home for about three hours, then turned around and came back!"[9]

THE 519TH PORT BATTALION

Supplying the war in Europe was an absolutely colossal undertaking. In 1942 a new division was created within the Army's Services of Supply. The Transportation Corps would handle the unloading of troops, movement of cargo, direct all rail and motor transport, and supervise ports. The loading and unloading of ships would be performed by Transportation Corps port battalions. Newly created for the war, the 519th Port Battalion was formed on April 1, 1943 and activated on June 25, 1943. It was composed of headquarters, the 302nd, 303rd, 304th, and 305th port companies. For nearly a month, eight officers and their staff waited for recruits to arrive and fill the empty barracks at Indiantown Gap Military Reservation. On July 19 the first large group—about 500 enlisted men—arrived by train from Camp Grant, an Army reception center in Illinois. On August 3, the second group arrived from Camp Upton, New York, swelling the battalion's ranks to over 1,000.[10] Cortland was among that second group. He was assigned to the 304th Port Company.

Corty took note of the varied backgrounds of the men that the Army had brought together. "It got a lot of different people to work together, which was interesting."[11] The Army's service units tended to include the youngest and the oldest men eligible for the service. Black men were thought to be unsuited for front lines fighting, so they found themselves in segregated units within the Transportation Corps. The 519th Port Battalion included men from two main regions. Half came from the Midwest, mostly from Wisconsin and Illinois. The others came from Mid-Atlantic states: New Jersey, New York, and Pennsylvania. There were guys from small towns and big cities. The 519th Port Battalion was filled primarily by the draft, but morale was high.

Dave Weaver, Bruce Kramlich, and John Shireman. (BCK)

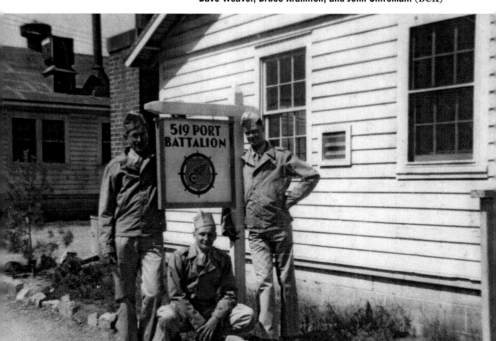

CAST OF CHARACTERS

The following men were either friends with Cortland, or were important contributors to the author's research:

Lawrence Botzon was born and raised in Chicago, Illinois. A year into his job at the Chicago, Milwaukee, St. Paul and Pacific Railroad he was drafted. He was only eighteen when he arrived at Indiantown Gap. Assigned to headquarters, his duty throughout the war would be to maintain records and occasionally serve guard duty (while on Utah Beach, Normandy).

James Dolan, from New York, was a staff sergeant in the 304th Port Company. He had volunteered in 1942 at age twenty six. James and Cortland became friends and bunked together during battalion travels. He was a well-liked older guy with a droll sense of humor and rapid speech.

Lawrence Botzon in Bristol, England, 1944. (BCK)

James Dolan at Camp McKay, Massachusetts, 1944. (BCK)

Mike "the Mouse" DeLaura was an Italian-American kid from upstate New York. He was a small but outspoken member of 304th Port Company. Late in the war DeLaura would be one of the few 519th men transferred to the Pacific before finally coming home.

Solomon Fein was at Indiantown Gap, but he was in a separate battalion from Cortland. Solomon was a member of the 301st Port Company, 518th Port Battalion. He trained at Indiantown Gap and worked in Boston at the same time as the 519th Port Battalion. He moved supplies in Fowey, England, and Utah Beach. While the 519th was in Antwerp, he served in nearby Gent. His experience was very similar to that of the 519th and was helpful to the author.

Solomon Fein and his friend "Oakie," 1944. (SF)

Mike DeLaura after his transfer to the 6th Army in the Pacific. (AMD)

Don Hartung was a 304th Port Company man from New Jersey. He and Cortland were friends and stayed in touch after the war.

Herbert Israel was drafted after graduating high school at nineteen. He was assigned to the 279th Port Company, 505th Port Battalion. His battalion did not train at Fort Indiantown Gap. It occupied Camp Myles Standish and worked Boston's docks in the summer before the 519th arrived there. The 505th was stationed in Morriston, Wales to work the port at Swansea. The 279th joined the 519th Port Battalion in May 1944, served at Utah Beach, then returned to the 505th in November 1944.

Bruce Kramlich was a nineteen-year-old college kid from Wisconsin. He was assigned to the 304th Port Company. At Indiantown Gap he, "had to get used to the regimentation of Army life. It wasn't fun, but it was what we had to do."[12] Later in Boston, Bruce was reassigned to battalion headquarters.

Bruce Kramlich at Indiantown Gap, 1943. (BCK)

Don Hartung in Normandy, 1944. (AJB)

John "Jack" Shireman was drafted from Richland Center, Wisconsin at age nineteen. He was assigned to the 304th Port Company. He recalled Indiantown Gap. "I thought it was desolate. Away from towns. We were trained to load and unload ships [the landships], rifle training, fitness, swimming, infiltration course and drilled."[13]

Peter Sloboda was drafted in April 1943 at age nineteen. A Brooklyn native, he had held an office job at General Bronze Corporation and was a recipient of the Navy "E" Award. He was assigned to the 280th Port Company. Like Herbert Israel's company, Peter's unit was originally part of the 505th Port Battalion and joined the 519th Port Battalion in May 1944. While the 279th parted ways in November 1944, Peter's 280th Port Company remained with the 519th until the end of the war.

John Shireman. (BCK)

Peter Sloboda in Mumbles, Wales in 1944. (PS)

Israel Sugarman at Tampico Flats in Antwerp, Belgium, 1945 or '46. (IS)

Ray Sonoski at Tampico Flats in Antwerp, Belgium, 1945 or '46. (BCK)

David Weaver in 1943. (DHW)

Alex Wanczak. (GW)

Ray Sonoski started in a completely different outfit but was transferred to the 304th Port Company. He offered his less than fond recollection of Indiantown Gap. *"Lovely place* [sarcasm]. It didn't look appetizing at all. Fortunately, I got in with a good bunch of boys."[14]

Israel "Irving" Sugarman was a 21-year-old from the Bronx, New York. He joined the military at an older age than most, because he had been caring for his dying father. "As soon as he died, I called to let the draft board know that I was available for the draft, and it didn't take long before I was drafted." While in the service he sent most of his salary home to his mother, keeping just enough to buy cigarettes. Irving married his sweetheart in September 1943. His wife rented a Boston apartment after the 519th moved there in October. In this way the newlyweds were able to see each other before Irving headed overseas.

Alex Wanczak had been a career Army man since 1935. A Pennsylvania native, he served with the 111 Engineer Battalion before reassignment to 519th Port Battalion headquarters. His photographs help to illustrate the 519th's story.

David Weaver was inducted into the Army a week after graduating from high school. Although he came from the same town as Bruce Kramlich, Wauwatosa, Wisconsin, the two didn't meet until joining the Army. They quickly became good friends. "I felt proud to join the Army. Basic training was hard work, but I found it interesting." He described his training. "We learned how to load big boxes of cinders, etc. on mock dry landships, then the next shift would unload the 'ships.'"[15] Weaver served in the 304th Port Company.

The NCOs (non-commissioned officers, i.e. sergeants and corporals) training the new recruits were Old Army, often veterans from the First World War. These soldiers were a tough bunch and were also, in Cortland's view, scornful of the inexperienced troops. Dave Weaver remembered one such NCO. "We had a S/Sgt named Elsmore, oldest guy in the 304th, Regular Army. He had been in the cavalry early in his career, and had been kicked in the jaw by an Army mule resulting in an offset lower jaw. He was a really nice guy, but not very tolerant of our greenhorn '90 day wonder' officers."[16]

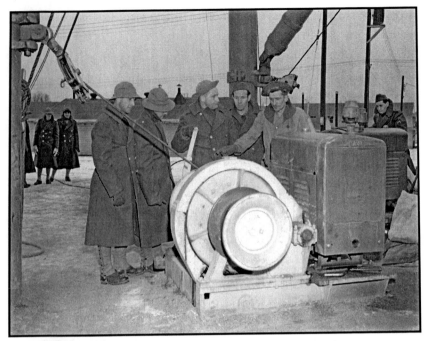

Instruction with a winch, Indiantown Gap Military Reservation, 1942. (USNA)

Instruction with a model ship, Indiantown Gap Military Reservation, 1942. (USNA)

One buck sergeant in the 304th is thought to have come from the famed 10th Light (later "Mountain") Division. Dave Weaver recalled: "His story was that he had been seriously injured falling while learning to ski! Probably a true story, as he had a definite limp."[17] This story does make sense. The Arkansas man had arrived from Camp McCoy, Wisconsin. This camp housed the Limited Service School founded in 1943 to train physically handicapped soldiers for specialist branches.

Cortland's time at Indiantown Gap was an adjustment to be sure. His first challenge was having to get up early in the morning. The author was surprised to hear this, so he asked, "Grandpa, don't you always get up early?" Corty responded, "Yeah, but I got up *earlier*! A band woke us up every morning, coming down the road playing music." He also joked that he was so skinny (140 lbs at 5ft. 6in.), because he didn't want to eat his mother's English cooking. Army food was not much better. While at Indiantown Gap Corty was introduced to an Army mess-hall favorite, creamed chipped beef served on toast. The men affectionately called it "shit on a shingle." He laughed when he recalled that Army food. "I'm always hungry, so to me it wasn't that bad." Another difference from Cortland's civilian life was the language—it could be foul. "I learned a few words I didn't know before!"[18]

TRAINING

Military training began on July 20th. Once basic training was completed the new recruits received technical training in port battalion work. The men were instructed in all the stevedoring skills necessary for handling military cargo. This included winch operation, rigging, stowing, checking, gear and tackle, mechanized equipment, warehousing, and a myriad of other responsibilities involved in port operation. The 519th's ranks included a few men who had worked as longshoremen in civilian life. Although at an advantage, they too needed instruction in the Army's unique procedures. There was classroom instruction and hands-on training on two artificial cargo ships and docks built on dry land. Port company work sections were divided into groups. Hatch and deck crews worked aboard the vessel. The wharf crew worked on the dock.[19]

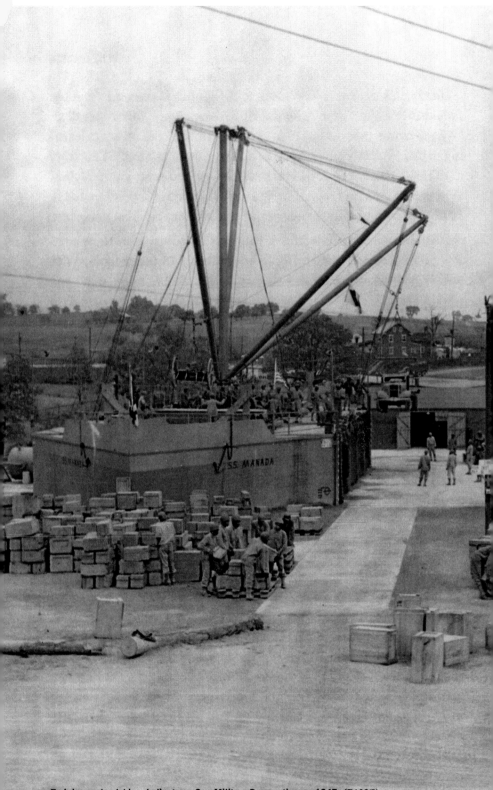

Training on landships, Indiantown Gap Military Reservation, c. 1945. (PANG)

The fort's landships and docks were an impressive sight. In August of 1943 two journalists were given a tour of Fort Indiantown Gap, reporting in The *Philadelphia Inquirer*:

> Months of special assignments to specialist branches of the
> armed services have accustomed us to meeting undreamed of
> innovations. But visiting a war-port wharf front, complete
> with quay, warehouses, rail sidings, besides which lay a pair of
> Liberty Ships miles from the ocean, on bone dry land was one of
> the most amazing sights we've seen to date.[20]

Supply work may have lacked the dash of the Air Force or the grit of combat, yet it would be a mistake to dismiss the contribution made by the war's military longshoremen. Personnel requirements set in the War Department's 1943 stevedore training manual offer insight into the valuable role of port battalion soldiers:

> Military stevedores must be physically capable of maintaining
> their top speed and highest peak of efficiency for extended
> periods. Ships may arrive at any time of day or night and must
> be loaded and unloaded in any kind of weather. The stevedore

A port company hatch crew preparing a pallet to hoist, Fort Indiantown Gap, 1942. (USNA)

Peeling potatoes, the classic Kitchen Police (KP) duty. Arthur J. Schroedter? (with bucket) and Mike DeLaura on the kitchen porch. September 3, 1943. (AMD)

must be good-natured and of rugged constitution to withstand the heavy and arduous work which he will be called upon to perform. He must posses the ability to make decisions swiftly, to think fast when confronted with the unexpected, and above all, he must be endowed with imagination and ingenuity. Every draft of cargo presents difficulties which must be solved quickly and efficiently. Many situations are unique, and it is the stevedore's responsibility to devise the most efficient means of dealing with them in the shortest possible time.[21]

Americans shared a feeling that all their servicemen were performing an important duty. After all, battles could not be fought without supplies. The 519th Port Battalion would not fight in the front lines, but noncombat service held its own dangers.

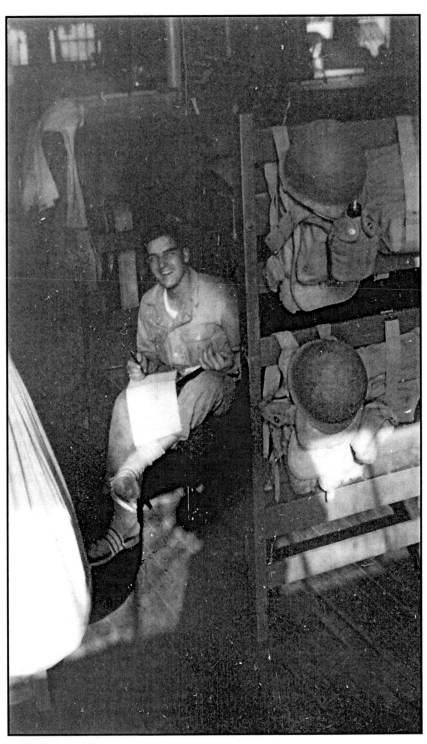

Bunks in the Cahill Building, Boston Army Base. (AMD)

4

BOSTON

On October 17, 1943 the battalion left Fort Indiantown Gap, arriving the next day at Camp Myles Standish, Massachusetts. Men who had not yet completed basic training resumed their courses firing on a rifle range. The battalion as a whole practiced firing the rifle grenade launcher. On the 25th the men were bussed and trucked to Boston Army Base. The port companies were housed in the Cahill Building (a warehouse) while HQ was set up in the Army Base Building. On November 14 the battalion relocated again, this time to Camp McKay, newly constructed in South Boston.[1] These new living quarters were an improvement.

The unit worked and trained in various facilities in the Port of Boston. They were instructed in driving equipment—various trucks, chisels (forklifts), tractors, and jeeps. Each company received a short training course aboard ships that were designated for use by the Army port battalions. The officers wanted further technical training for their men. However, due to Boston's labor shortage the men of the 519th instead spent much of their time assisting the civilian longshoremen and the city's permanent transportation troops. The civilian workers would sometimes stop work due to rain or cold weather. These breaks gave the GIs the opportunity to use the docks for the practice of loading live cargo in realistic conditions.

Overall the higher-ups were less than happy about their stay in Boston. Officers complained that the civilian workers encouraged their

soldiers to "slow up" and "take it easy." There was little time for technical training, and the city did not offer adequate space for military training.[2]

Cortland's days consisted mainly of loading ammunition and other supplies and delivering trucks to the dock. He and some other drivers would be transported to Fort Devons where they picked up trucks and drove them back to the port to be shipped overseas. He had his driver's license before enlisting, but "we had to learn the Army way."[3] The Army's 2½-ton GMC Jimmy, or "deuce and a half" as it was called, was indeed a change from a typical civilian truck. It had ten gears, requiring double-clutching. There were also numerous confusing knobs and levers.[4] Corty's driving instructor tried to teach him how—at certain speeds—he could switch gears without using the clutch. He gave it a try, and "I ground every gear in the truck!" Cortland also spent time driving forklifts or yard tractors. "We brought boxes to big cranes which someone loaded on the ships."[5]

In December Cortland was assigned an excellent job. He delivered mail for the city of Boston. With all the young men headed to war, the US Post Office was understaffed. During the busy Christmas season Corty and a local high school teen drove around town making deliveries. Corty's favorite destination was 495 Summer Street. Working here

at the First Naval District were the WAVES, "Women Accepted for Volunteer Emergency Service." The Navy women were apparently quite fond of our Corty. When he showed up

with a delivery they always invited him to stay for a sandwich and coffee. He made a point of dropping off the kid early so he could chat up the ladies.

A considerably less enjoyable and more common assignment was guard duty. One night Cortland was patrolling the base when a wise-guy officer suddenly leapt out of the shadows. Startled, Corty swung up his carbine, nearly shooting the officer. He had not pulled the trigger, but the officer was pretty steamed. "He turned white as a sheet!" The gun's safety was not on, which was against regulations. As punishment, the angered officer restricted Cortland to the barracks. He figured the officer was testing his level of alertness, but it seems more likely that the guy thought it would be amusing to spook one of the guards. His confinement to the barracks didn't stick. The man in charge of checking passes was a buddy, so he let Corty head out to town despite the infraction.[7] There was a subway station not far from Camp McKay (Columbia Station), so it was easy to get downtown and to the USO club for music, dancing, and movies.

John Shireman recalled the work in Boston. "I had authorization to drive anything but combat vehicles. So, I was driving sergeants and other officers around on docks a lot. When we got to Boston I was working a six-ton chisel. We'd stack 4 x 4 foot boxes in trucks. We had a bunch of hairy experiences, because it was in the winter and those things had slick tires. There was no tread to them. If you accelerated you just spun. We had a guy come roaring out of the warehouse with a bunch of bombs, and he dropped them on the dock. They were just cold [not armed]. These were 1,000 pound bombs, and we were just trying to stack them as high as we could. A friend of mine went to back his chisel up and then he put the brakes on. It didn't do any good. The chisel and all went down to the bottom of the harbor! They fished him out between the boat and the dock. Another guy was going through a doorway and didn't get the blades down fast enough, and the chisel went right up in the air." The fork blades impaled the wall above the door frame and continued their downward movement, which pulled the forklift off the ground. "There he was sitting up there with the wheels running."[8]

In December of 1943 the Army sought to improve the enlisted men's morale by immediately raising the ranks of non-commissioned officers. For instance, a corporal would be moved up to become a sergeant. This opened NCO positions for privates.[9] Private Cortland Hopkins was made technician 5th grade, a rank nearly equivalent to corporal in the infantry. Put into effect in 1942, the technicians were a new category of NCO.

Weaver and Kramlich at Camp McKay, 1943 or '44. (BCK)

To reflect his specialized skills, the Tech/5 had the same pay as a corporal, but he ranked just below a corporal in the chain of command. Corty explained his promotion. "There was a bulletin board that we checked every day for our duties. I was up for Tech/5." The company needed the position filled, so Corty was notified to take the necessary advanced training. He gladly accepted the promotion. His pay went from $50 per month as private to $66. Much later in Antwerp, Belgium, he was also offered a promotion to Tech/4. Cortland, however, quickly declined. "I gave it five seconds thought." His civilian work experience had left him wary of management positions. He viewed the higher rank as "just extra responsibility," not worth the $12 raise.[10]

John O'Connor, 304th Port Co. clerk and friend of Cortland at Camp McKay, 1943 or '44. (BCK)

Cortland's technician 5th grade shoulder patch. Shown at 50%. (AJB)

Cortland photographed in 1943 or '44. (AJB)

5

THE ATLANTIC

On March 23, 1944 the 519th Port Battalion boarded the troop-ship SS *Edmund B. Alexander* at Commonwealth Pier, Boston. They left port on the 24th. Navy ships accompanied the transport to offer protection from German U-boats.[1] Their ship was an ex-German passenger liner captured in WWI. Its state rooms had been stripped out to provide quarters for the thousands of troops. Upon boarding, Cortland was shown to his cabin and given the choice of top or bottom bunk. Whoever it was making this offer figured anybody would prefer the bottom, but Corty picked the top. He told the guy, "If I'm on the bottom, and the guy above me throws up, I'll get sprayed. This way if I get sick, I'll spray someone else."[2] People were definitely getting sick.

On the first day at sea the battalion was assembled on the top deck. The commanding officer was about to address the men. The waves rocked the ship as he spoke, and suddenly everybody ran to the rail on one side of the ship to throw up. Irving Sugarman joked, "We almost capsized the ship!"[3] Cortland remembered GIs slipping on the slick floor. "The deck looked like a skating rink!"[4] Most everyone's stomach calmed down after a day or two. John Shireman added, "All I can say is the ocean was rough. Lots of us got ill. I don't think I ate more than a half dozen times."[5]

Bruce Kramlich offered his own description of the voyage. "We were part of a large convoy leaving for England. We had lots of Navy ships (destroyer escorts) constantly going all around the boats in the con-

voy. They were to protect the convoy from German subs. All the boats would change course at the same time. All communication between boats was by semaphore." Sema-

USAT *Edmund B. Alexander* (US Army Transport) exiting Boston Harbor, Massachusetts, January 6, 1945. (NHF)

phores are signals sent by flashing light. Communication by radio would attract the attention of enemy U-boats. "Our bunks on the boat were three and four high. I did get sick one day when we were having a life boat drill. It was a nice day with big rolling waves."[6]

The ship was overcrowded, so much so that there was time to feed all the men only twice a day. Schedule cards were handed out to organize the meal times. The troops went either to the top deck or second area below to be served their food. It was standing-room only. "We had to eat out of our shit-skillet."[7] Their mess tins were so named because of the way the food was slopped together in an unappealing muck.

The ship also carried women—nurses who had their cabins on the promenade. The officers onboard were quartered on the same deck, separated only by a hallway. Naturally, there was some fraternization. To put an end to that problem, the higher-ups decided the ladies needed to be guarded. Cortland was put on guard duty one evening. "I heard the [officers'] showers running, so I knew there would be action that night. A guy walked up, wearing only a pair of shorts." He tried to get through, but Corty denied him, telling the officer to "Go take a cold shower!"

The author asked Corty why he felt so comfortable using such an informal tone with a superior officer. He wasn't worried about it, because the officer "had no authority. I had the authority in that situation!" Cortland was happy to serve his country, but he was not too keen on the stricter military formalities. To an extent, he and his fellows could get by without adhering to proper military courtesy. There was some understanding that these were not career soldiers. Cortland provided another anecdote to illustrate. "One of the guys was rolling barrels. An officer came up. He didn't like the way he was doing it. He told him to *lift* the barrels. The private said, 'I think it's easier to do it my way.' The officer said, 'You're not supposed to think!' So, the guy says, 'It's *my* back, *I'll* do the thinking!'"[8]

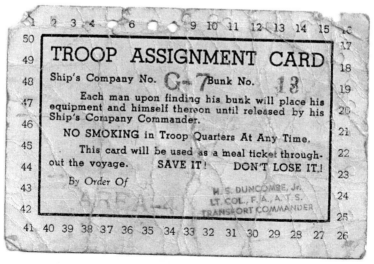

Troop assignment card / meal ticket from the 519th Port Battalion's voyage aboard the *Edmund B. Alexander*. (BCK)

519th Port Bn. HQ at Pitch & Pay House on Pitch & Pay Lane, Stoke Bishop. (BCK)

Captain F. W. Coykendall and Lieutenant Perkins on the patio at headquarters. (BCK)

6

ENGLAND

The transport ship arrived in Liverpool on April 5, 1944.[1] Of immediate interest to the Americans were the many barrage balloons floating above the city. "They must be holding the island up!" Corty joked.[2] Tethered with steel cables, these great balloons floated above the city as a deterrent to enemy bombers. The 304th Port Company stayed at transit camp #4 in Huyton, an eastern suburb of Liverpool.[3] There were inadequate preparations for feeding the large number of men coming into the city. Dave Weaver explained the food situation. Many of the men threw away their kitchen food and secretly ate rations that were meant to be saved for the field. "Everybody had rations. They had K-rations, which are like a Cracker Jack box, full of stuff. When we landed in Liverpool our food was terrible. We got to opening up—skillfully opening up—that package and getting the food out and putting sand or something in. They [officers] could tell by picking it up, if it felt right. They never caught us that I know of."[4]

They left Huyton, taking a train to Camp Sea Mills in Shirehampton, Bristol. They arrived on April 11. Army installations were bulging with GIs at that time, so many men were billeted in private homes in Bristol's suburbs, Sea Mills and Stoke Bishop.[5] Of the three million US troops coming through Britain during the course of the war only 100,000 were billeted in private homes. In his book *A Moment in History*, author Bryan Morse describes the billeting process. Although he writes of the Rhondda area of Wales, the procedure in Bristol was likely

Marvin, Weaver, and Kramlich with their host family, the Elliotts. Stoke Bishop, Bristol. (BCK)

identical. A local police officer or British soldier would go through the neighborhoods inspecting houses. If a family had a spare room available, then wartime regulations required they take in an American. The host family was told something to the effect of, "You'll take two Yanks," and the officer later returned with a truck full of GIs.

The English were actually rather nervous about the whole affair, because they expected these Americans to be a rough and tumble bunch. Hollywood's gangster and western films informed this prejudice. As the Americans were introduced to their new homes the hosts were relieved to see how friendly the boys actually were. In fact, when neighbors met they liked to brag about who had the most polite guests. Some Americans expected a cold welcome from the supposedly reserved English, but they were pleased to find their hosts warm and inviting. The authorities made an effort to place officers in the upper-class homes of lawyers, doctors, etc. Enlisted men were billeted with working-class families.[6]

The accommodations were for sleeping only. Early in the morning the soldiers headed out to work, camp, or training. They returned in the evening. The troops were instructed not to eat their host family's food. Civilian rationing was very strict, while the Army had food in abundance. Ray Sonoski's host family insisted on sharing their evening meal "My friend Red Ruidl lived around the corner from me. The two of us would stay outside at night to avoid going in the house at supper time. They would come out and invite us in, and we kept refusing. So, finally one day he [their host] says, 'Why won't you come in and have something with us?' So we had to tell him the truth, that we weren't allowed. 'Well, let me tell you,' he says. 'If I didn't have anything to serve you, I wouldn't ask you. I want you to come in and have something.' So, from then on it was almost a nightly ritual. We had to go in and have something to eat. We were eating things that weren't available even to the military—tomatoes and eggs and that sort of thing."[7]

Cortland and his platoon sergeant, James Dolan, were billeted with a very nice family who "brought us tea and crumpets every morning."[8] There were German bombing raids in Bristol in the early morning hours.[9] John Shireman noted, "Bristol was a nice clean town. We were billeted in a very nice home. When the air raids came the lady of the house would call us downstairs for tea and crumpets."[10] Some host families had a bomb shelter in their backyards. Here they would wait until the all-clear sounded. The last bombing raid was on May 15th.[11]

Cortland had a very pleasant relationship with his English host family, but elsewhere in urban areas—London in particular—American public behavior was met with general disapproval from the locals. Corty relayed a common saying by the English: "The trouble with the Yanks is that they're overpaid, oversexed, and over here!" The Americans' reply was: "The trouble with the Limies is they're underpaid, undersexed, and under Eisenhower!"[12] (General Eisenhower was supreme commander of all Allied forces.) Many Americans were indeed drinking, womanizing, and even fighting. The US troops were better paid than

304th Port Co. men at Blaise Castle, Bristol. Herb Koller (no hat), Dick Justice (far right). (AJB)

their British counterparts, and beer was readily available to the young men. While British boys were largely absent, lonely girls flocked to the Americans in their sharp uniforms. Although Cortland's battalion was all white, seventy percent of the men in the US Army's Transportation Corps were black.[13] The African-American servicemen were welcomed by the British. Indeed, their skin color was of little concern to girls looking for dates to the local dances. Sadly, these couplings sparked fights between white and black Americans. Cortland was unaware of any violence during his stay, but it seems Bristol did have its share of race-motivated fighting.[14] Wartime security banned the media from reporting on such embarrassments. The 519th Port Battalion men interviewed by the author had not witnessed such race violence, but John Shireman explained that racism wasn't the only issue sparking fights. "There were fights between white guys too for various reasons. They get to drinking, you know, and it takes over."[15]

The battalion began working at the Avonmouth Docks on April 13.[16] Cortland's company helped pack and load materials for the upcoming invasion. Dave Weaver briefly described the work. "We were working fairly hard. I don't know if we had twelve hour shifts or what it was, but I know we were loading up small coastal ships and that kind of thing to prepare for the invasion."[17] An article in *The Stars and Stripes* on May 20, 1944 sets the scene in an unnamed British port:

Some of the hardest and most dangerous work being done on this side of the fighting lines is performed by the U.S. Army's Transportation Corps stevedores who make up the port battalions toiling on the docks and in the warehouses of the great ports of the British Isles.

Enthusiasm goes up when the cargo being taken off smacks loudly of the battlefront. Virtually all the men prefer unloading military equipment with high priority, such as Thunderbolts and blockbusters, to foodstuffs and other articles.

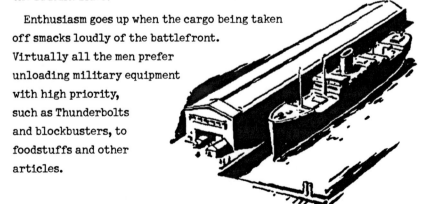

Broken arms, smashed fingers and legs and numerous other
injuries speak for the hazardous nature of the work. Often a
steel cable snaps and the broken strand swings wildly down,
slashing anything in its path.

Sometimes the little tow trucks which cart the cargo from
wharf to warehouse topple over the side of the quay, driver
and all.

The role of the port battalions in the coming great battle for
the liberation of Europe is being planned by those charged with
directing operations. Certain port units are receiving training
for amphibious operations. Making extensive use of amphibious
trucks, they will provide supplies for the men who establish the
beachheads.[18]

John Shireman remembered the hard work and the danger. "You
were sweating. You were really working! We loaded all the stuff on the
ships in Boston, and we went over there to England and unloaded it.
When we were working on getting the stuff ready for the beach [Normandy] I got my ankle jammed down in one of the conveyors that was
bringing the rations down. It was so heavy that I couldn't keep it off of
me and one of the things came down on me and caught my ankle in
there and twisted it pretty bad. I was out for about two or three weeks.
They put me in the infirmary for a while because I couldn't walk. I
spent most of the time writing letters."[19]

One day after a hard shift Irving Sugarman was encouraged by his
sergeant to volunteer for an overtime assignment. That evening at the
docks Irving and Irwin Tobe moved crates of ammunition. They had
been at work for some time when the city's air-raid siren went off. The
Germans were bombing the city again. Tobe ran for the shelter of a
nearby truck. He yelled back, "Hey Shug! Get in here where it's safe!"
Irving started to run over, then he took a look at the label on the truck:
"Explosives." The truck was packed full of ammunition—hardly the
safest shelter. They were fortunate no bombs landed in the area.[20]

There were civilian longshoremen to do some of the work, so Cortland and some others in his company spent more of their time in
training. Although there were sufficient numbers, the Brits available

to work the port tended to be old and less than efficient. The bulk of Britain's young fit men were at war. The US Army's official history of the war makes mention of their peculiar work habits:

> Americans found it hard to appreciate the British custom of taking "tea breaks" in the morning and afternoon. When the dockers took the break first and were followed a little later by the crane workers, operations might be halted from forty minutes to an hour, since the dockers could not function without cranes.[21]

There was some leisure time for the 304th Port Company. Rather than heading into the city, the men tended to stay in the Bristol suburbs. Cortland described how they became regulars at a local pub: "We went to a place called 'The Black Swan.' We called it 'The Dirty Duck.'" Guinness Stout was the drink of choice. Corty was amused by the long-handled English taps. "It's funny, you go into these places, and they have these long handles for the beer. The beer was warm! I guess they didn't make the beer cold until after the GIs came." Cold or not, the beer flowed freely. Drunk Americans stumbling home at night were liable to be picked up by the local authorities. "Our CO [commanding officer] didn't want that. He liked his beer too. He appointed MPs [military police] to help the guys back to their barracks, instead of jail or the stockade. I never drank too much, so I could find my way back."[22]

With the tremendous secrecy surrounding the planned invasion, none of the enlisted men knew where the landing would be. Up until early May of 1944 the Allies had yet to defeat the Germans and Italians in the Desert War. Consequently, Cortland had not even considered France. "I thought we would be going to North Africa."[23] No matter which invasion point, he had little cause for anxiety about the impending battle. Many 519th Port Battalion men simply assumed their duty was to remain in England to manage the outgoing supplies. That view, however, would quickly change.

On April 28, 1944 several hundred men from the 1st Engineer Special Brigade were killed or wounded during Exercise Tiger, a rehearsal for the invasion of Utah Beach. From April 22nd to the 30th, 4th Infantry Division troops and the supporting 1st ESB units had gathered in England's Lyme Bay. The practice beach, Slapton Sands, was physically very similar to the invasion point in France. A fleet of crowded ships gathered offshore to engage in the mock invasion. After dark on April 27th, about a dozen German *Schnellboote* (known as "E-Boats" to the Allies) slipped into the bay and attacked the poorly protected landing ships. Two LSTs (Landing Ship, Tank) were sunk and a third was badly damaged. Several hundred Americans were killed.[24] The survivors were ordered to keep quiet, but rumor of the disaster quickly spread to the port companies back in Bristol.

It occurred to Cortland that there was a real possibility of his outfit joining the invasion as replacements. Indeed, the 519th Port Battalion was subsequently attached to the 1st Engineer Special Brigade. The timing led Cortland and others in his company to the conclusion that they would not have taken part in the Normandy invasion were it not for the losses at Slapton Sands. However, this was not the case. Army records show that the lost 1st ESB men had been replaced not by the 519th, but by an Army Quartermaster Service company and a Quartermaster Railhead company.[25] Discharging the invasion fleet's equipment, vehicles, and supplies had always been the plan for the 519th. The battalion commander, Major Charles H. Nabors, was well aware of their planned involvement in Operation NEPTUNE. This was the Allies' secret code name describing the cross-channel assault phase of Operation OVERLORD, the code name for the invasion of Europe through the beaches of northwestern France.

Major Nabors had attempted to include his port companies in the practice exercises taking place on England's coast, but was unsuccessful.[26] There was a very limited window for the invasion training. Priority had been given to the Force U units, those hitting Utah Beach with the first waves of assault troops. The port battalions were Force B units, support troops scheduled to land just after the initial assault.[27] They would have to do without special amphibious training and rely only on the supply-handling skills developed on Bristol's docks. The average GI was privy to none of these details, but by May it was made clear that the 519th was joining the invasion. Officers and NCOs were briefed on lessons learned from the amphibious exercises, and the enlisted men went through a brief period of physical training. With the invasion date fast approaching, Cortland and his comrades were considered ready for action.

7
THE INVASION

Two additional companies joined the 519th Port Battalion shortly before the Normandy invasion. The 280th Port Company was attached on May 4, 1944 and the 279th Port Company on May 13. They were originally part of the 505th Port Battalion.[1] It was in the latter half of May that General Eisenhower ordered all troops taking part in Operation OVERLORD/NEPTUNE to their marshalling areas on England's south coast. The average soldier still did not know that Normandy was the target. On May 31 the battalion left Bristol, marching to a train station in the suburb of Avonmouth.[2] The train cars were crammed with troops, so Corty had the good fortune to get bumped up to the officers' car. Unlike the enlisted men, the officers had coffee, which they were kind enough to share.

The men arrived at the US Army Marshalling Area Camp 139, APO 134, at Bridgend, Wales. The bulk of soldiers assembling for the invasion were living in pyramid-like tents. These were nicknamed "sausage camps" because of their appearance on maps as linked blobs. Cortland's battalion, however, was housed in barrack buildings. To ensure the secrecy of this sensitive operation, Army MPs confined the men to camp. "They closed the gate and locked us in. I knew this assignment was important because they took our ID away and gave us tags. We had to address the card to our next of kin and tie it to our bag."[3] There were movies and games to pass the time. As John Shireman put it, "The Army is very good at waiting."[4] Cortland vividly remembered a

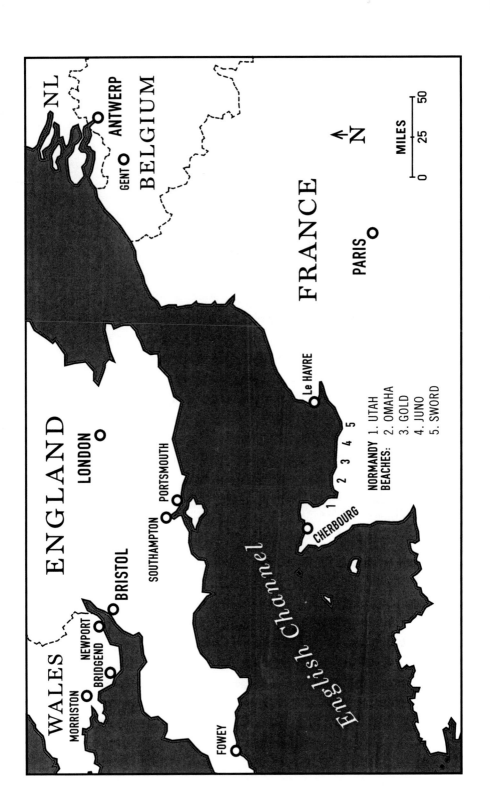

baseball game put on by the 304th Port Company. Some of the players would not survive the invasion.

After two weeks it was finally time to ship out. "We got ammo, three days of K-rations, and a carton of cigarettes." Cortland's favorite brand had been Wings, "the cheapest I could get."[5] In the Army, he could enjoy the brands considered to be the best. Troops were issued new fatigues that were saturated with a chemical paste to block out poison gas. It wasn't known if the Germans would resort to using this terrible weapon. The antigas uniforms were stiff, had a foul odor, and were unpleasantly greasy to the touch. The US Army planned to issue these to its entire invasion force, but it seems distribution was incomplete in the port companies. The men were given French money, seasickness tablets (which were useless), and water purification tablets. A blue arc was painted on the front of their helmets to signify their attachment to the 1st Engineer Special Brigade.

On June 2 the 519th Port Battalion left the marshalling area and arrived at Newport, Wales. The 303rd Port Company split from the rest of the battalion and embarked at Bristol and Southampton, England.[6] The officers directed the men to the ships. "My sergeant was there to make sure you got on the boat. He'd call out your first name, you'd call out your second." Their packs were reviewed before boarding. "One guy had filled his gas mask with candy. He said it was his 'shacking-up material'!"[7] The battalion was divided among numerous waiting Liberty Ships, freighters, and coasters. They remained anchored until late in the evening of June 5th. It was only while en route to France that the men were officially informed of their destination. The 519th would be invading an area code named "Utah Beach" in Normandy. As the men were informed of this they received General Eisenhower's Order of the Day, a letter to inspire the troops.

By 2:30 A.M., June 6th, the Allied convoy was taking position to make their landing on the enemy-held beach. The ships anchored twelve miles from shore, a distance beyond the range of German artillery.[8] The responsibility of the 519th was to transport supplies into the beach after it was taken. The unit was not expected to land on the beach until the following day.

Cortland spent that early morning pacing about the deck and chatting with the other GIs. He wandered up to a group of guys he didn't know. "They had a 'T' and 'O' [unit insignia] painted on their helmets. I asked a kid what it stood for."[9] It was a group of the 90th Infantry Division. Texas and Oklahoma contributed all the men to this unit in the first World War. By WWII the 90th Infantry drew men from all across the States, so the 'T' and 'O' were then more associated with the division's nickname, the "Tough 'Ombres." As participants in the initial assault on Normandy, these men would have been part of either the 1st or 3rd Battalion in the 359th Infantry Regiment.[10] "When I saw that they were infantry, I knew this was serious."

Cortland realized he must have strayed from his unit's area of the ship, but he decided to stick around, because the guys had offered to share their stew. They were heating cans on the ship's hot steam pipes. As they ate an officer shouted at Cortland, telling him to untuck his leggings and pull out his shirt. Cortland was a bit puzzled, but did as he was told. "Who the hell is *he*?" Corty grumbled to a young soldier next to him. The soldier replied, "You better listen to him, he's been to North Africa."[11] Having experienced the amphibious landings in German-held North Africa, this veteran officer realized how dangerous the gas-proof uniforms could be. The treatment that made their clothes resistant to gas attack also made them watertight. When a man stepped out of the boat, water flowed over his belt, and into the legs of his trousers, where it was trapped. That weight, added to the already heavy equipment, drowned many a soldier.

Cortland looked around at the combat troops and started to wonder, "what the hell am I doing here?" The public address system came on, announcing the start of the invasion. The "Tough 'Ombres" started climbing down the rope ladder on the side of the ship, loading into the small landing craft in the waters below. Cortland took this as his cue to move on. As he was walking against the crowd that same 90th Infantry Division officer spotted Cortland and ordered him into the craft. "But, I'm not infantry!" Corty protested. The officer barked back, "You are now, soldier. Get your ass in the boat!"[12] Perhaps the officer was making sure the landing craft was full when it went in. Maybe he thought Cortland actually *was* a combat infantryman trying to chicken out. All soldiers had removed marks of rank and unit insignia from their uniforms to aid in the secrecy of the operation, so some confusion was possible. An officer could still be identified by the vertical white stripe painted on the rear of his helmet. In any case, this officer was geared-up for battle and in no mood for arguments. Cortland followed orders and clambered down to join the soldiers in the waiting LCVP (Landing Craft, Vehicle or Personnel). The port company man was thrown in with the fighting men.

During the three-and-a-half-hour ride all the men could do was wait, worry, and get seasick. Thankfully, Cortland did not get ill. "I was in pretty good shape, I guess." The craft hit a sandbar and came to a sudden halt. "The officers were all swearing, because we were stuck there and the Germans were shooting at us with 88s." The craft was meant to unload closer to the beach, but it stuck on the sand bar with artillery shells falling all around as the door was lowered. The men plunged into the water. As a kid, Corty had taken swimming lessons with his church group at Lake George, New York. As a teenager he had

Concrete German gun emplacement on Utah Beach. (DHW)

received lifeguard training. This skill proved most useful in his situation. Some unfortunate men didn't know how to swim at all. "We were in over our heads, but I wasn't worried. I had a life preserver on and I knew how to swim." That life preserver turned out to be no help. It was only after he was standing on the beach that he thought to inflate it. Cortland remembered everyone from his craft made it to shore, but "a lot of guys panicked and drowned."[13]

Cortland and some thirty "Tough 'Ombres" hit the beach that morning, probably no earlier than 10:00 A.M.[14] Bullets whizzed by and explosions threw sand in the air. Corty kept pace for awhile, but was left behind. "They had maps, see, and they all went off somewhere."[15] For a few moments Cortland was left on the beach, but he didn't have to wait long for direction. Another group of infantry came up from behind and pulled Corty with them. "We went up on the hill and waited 'till they cleared the mines. I lobbed a couple grenades in a pill box. A guy brought up a pole charge and blew the door open. My carbine jammed. An officer told me, 'See that GI? Take his. He won't be needing it anymore.' From then on it was kind of foggy."

Corty took the weapon from the dead soldier and moved on. He hunkered down behind some cover, and fired off some rounds. Eventually the shooting stopped. "I did enough fighting for what I wanted to do." During the fight Corty's hand had been grazed by a piece of flying shrapnel, but it went untreated. "When I got to the medic I saw there were a lot of guys a lot worse off than me, so I just left."[16] It's unclear how long Cortland was separated from the 519th. Some time later he bumped into a sergeant from his own unit and rejoined his company. He would no longer be directly involved in fighting, but that certainly did not mean he was out of danger.

Cortland posing with his M1 carbine in a Utah Beach apple orchard. Note the onyx ring given to him by his girlfriend, Marge. Late June 1944. (AJB)

Major Charles H. Nabors (on right) standing by a knocked-out German tank on Utah Beach. (BCK)

8

UTAH BEACH DANGERS

As the very first wave of infantrymen hit the beach, their officers began to look for the landmarks that they had so carefully studied back in England. It became clear that their landing craft had drifted one mile south from the intended invasion point. There was only one general on the beach with the initial assault companies, Brigadier General Theodore Roosevelt (son of President Theodore Roosevelt). He and the other officers quickly made the decision to fight inland from there, rather than direct subsequent assaults at the originally planned landing zone to the north. The mislanding was actually quite fortuitous, as that area of Utah Beach would turn out to be the least defended. Colonel Eugene Caffey, the deputy commander of the 1st Engineer Special Brigade, was also on the beach in that first wave. He met with Roosevelt and radioed the Navy to continue landing the 1st ESB there. His engineers had spent weeks planning their operations for the particular landscape to the north, but they would adjust and tackle the obstacles on this unfamiliar beach.[1]

MINES

Roads and fields had been thoroughly mined by the Germans, yet few were found on the beach itself. On D-Day the 1st Engineer Special Brigade men had the dangerous job of marking and then removing these deadly obstacles. Forty-five thousand would eventually be cleared from the whole of Utah Beach.[2] It was a long-term undertaking. The

port company men were careful to avoid the cordoned-off areas await-
ing clearance. In the first week on the beach an unfortunate farm horse
strayed into a minefield adjacent to the 304th Port Company's bivouac
area.[3] The grisly result was a reminder of the hidden danger waiting
beyond the engineers' white tape.

SNIPERS

German snipers were a problem in the first few days of landing. John
Shireman discussed this hazard. "When we came inland they said
there were still snipers. There were guys up in trees that were trying
to pick off the officers. That's why they took all the insignia off their
uniform. I saw a whole bunch of green officers coming in, a whole
truckload of them. All their bars were glinting up, and I thought,
'Mmmm man you're going to be putting those bars in your pocket.'"[4]
Those shiny bars were marks of rank and would attract any snipers in
the area.

Cortland witnessed none other than General Omar Bradley repri-
manding one of the 304th Port Company sergeants for ignoring the
threat. "We were on the beach. We had our tin hats [steel helmets]
tucked under our arms and our sergeant didn't know it. Bradley came
driving by in his jeep, saw us, found the sergeant, and started chewing
him out. I couldn't hear what was being said, because I was too far
away, but saw the sergeant's head bobbing up and down like a cork,
'Yes, yes, yes!' There was no saluting because of the danger of snipers
nearby."[5]

FIGHTER BOMBERS

On the evening of June 9th, members of the 304th Port Company
were finishing a day's work on the SS *Charles Morgan*. They had been
unloading the ship's cargo and were to remain on board to complete
their job in the morning. Having spent the past several nights in stuffy
cabins below deck, Irving Sugarman joined a group that decided to
sleep on the top deck. They brought up their blankets and pillows to
lay under the night sky. Others thought this position was too exposed
and opted to return to their bunks below.

In the early morning hours of June 10th their ship was struck by a German dive-bomber.[6] The bomb dropped straight down the hatch, exploding at the bottom of the hold.[7] The walls of the ship blew out, killing and injuring a dozen men from the company. Landing craft quickly arrived to collect the survivors. It was still dark as men abandoned the sinking ship. They were motored to shore and the front door dropped down. Sugarman remembered that the first guy out of the craft stepped off the ramp and disappeared beneath the surface of the water. "Chico" was a short guy, no more than five feet. Thinking it was shallow water, he had plunged down into an underwater crater left by German artillery. "We were so shocked to see that happen, but he came up alright."[8]

The June 10th Morning Report from the 304th Port Company listed four men killed and six men wounded or injured on the 10th due to "enemy bombing of ship."[9] A later report records three men as missing that day and presumed dead.[10] This was especially sobering for Israel. His friend Frank Rodriguez was among those killed. The two were bunk-mates aboard the ship and had been billeted together in England. It seems very likely that the SS *Charles Morgan* was the same ship that transported Cortland across the English Channel. His company was present on the *Charles Morgan,* and it carried troops from the 90th Infantry Division. Having been mixed up with the departing infantry on June 6th, Cortland was not on board during the attack. He didn't know the casualties personally, but it disheartened him to think these guys had been playing baseball just a few days prior at the marshalling area in Britain.

Dave Weaver offered his recollection of the German fighter planes. "We did experience enemy aircraft activity the first two days while still aboard ship. I remember fighter plane battles above us, in fact I recall hearing bullets bouncing off the steel deck of the ship, and thinking, 'Gee, this is just like in the newsreels!' So I had to duck back under the overhead! And I remember the fighter plane flying over us at night."[11]John Shireman added to this particular anecdote, "We got strafed a couple times on boats in the harbor. I remember one time when Weaver was working the winch and they started strafing. Bullets

Liberty Ship *Charles Morgan* down at the stern off
Utah Beach on June 10, 1944, after she was hit by
a German bomb. LCT-474 is alongside. (NHF)

were bouncing right off the hoist poles. The guys were all complaining, because there's no place to dig a hole on a steel ship! We were all jumping in coils of rope!"[12]

The 519th Port Battalion bivouacked on Utah Beach. (BCK)

Shireman recounted how the beach itself was frequently attacked by enemy fighter planes. "We were coming in from work late at night and we didn't have any lights on. This Stuka [a German dive-bomber] was flying down the beach, and we had just come in [on a DUKW]. They told us to make a run for the seawall and dig in. We were coming off of duty, and all we had were our helmet liners. So, we were digging with them. We could hear bullets bouncing off the wall."[13] One particular fighter plane was famous among the men working on Utah Beach. This German fighter strafed the beach nightly. He came with such regularity that the GIs nicknamed the plane "the 3 o'clock alarm."[14]

At the end of a day's work the men came home to their foxholes. Initially the men were dug in about 300 yards inland from the seawall. The holes were several feet deep and were wide enough to hold two men. Although covered with a pup tent, they were still exposed to the elements. The men tried to shelter their foxholes with dunnage, spare pieces of wood left over from packing. Discarded inflatable life preservers were collected from the beach and used as cushions. One evening Cortland was huddled in his foxhole with German fighter-bombers in the sky. He thought to himself, "I could be home in a gin mill, drinking a beer. But I'm over here getting bombed!"[15]

Sleeping in a foxhole offered protection, but it was dreadfully uncomfortable. Sand was always sliding in on the soldiers. It really poured down when the ground shook from American antiaircraft artillery or nearby bomb blasts. In a 1994 newspaper interview Matt Marvin reported three young men in his area were killed after trying to sleep above ground. They had evidently become frustrated with their cramped, sandy holes. A sudden explosion showered them with shrapnel. They died before anyone could stop the bleeding.[16]

John Shireman had his own close call. "I was buried in my foxhole when we took a direct hit from a Stuka. I had large boards over the top to protect from shrapnel. Our tent was blown away, and my jacket—which I used for a pillow—was burned."[17] The walls of sand collapsed on him, covering his chest and legs. He couldn't dig himself out, but he also did not want to risk anyone's life by calling for help. "I couldn't move. I never yelled out because I was OK—I could still breathe. I just laid there and went to sleep. A sergeant came by the next morning and he pulled me out."[18] One evening Irving Sugarman suffered a similar shock. Disoriented after an explosion, Irving found he could not move his legs. He looked down in a panic, but they weren't there. For a terror-filled moment he thought they had been blown off. He was endlessly relieved to realize they had only been buried under the sand.[19]

Bruce Kramlich described the aerial bombing on headquarters' area of the beach. "We had several air raids while we were on the beach. The worst one was on June 15, 1944 when five bombs were dropped in our area and several of our troops were killed. We were also shelled by German 88s, but they never did any damage to our area of the beach."[20] The 519th Port Battalion operations reports provide more detail:

> The only Battalion battle casualties were suffered during the first week of landing operations on the continent. All were victims of aerial bombing. Of the total number of casualties (22) there were 10 killed and 12 wounded. Casualties occurred both aboard the ship where sections were working and in the bivouac area.[21]

THE TENSION

For seven weeks the port companies moved supplies under continuous threat from the Germans. In addition to suffering night attacks by aircraft, the American positions were shelled during the day by German artillery farther inland. It was a mere twenty miles to the front lines, and in some places the German forces were no more than five miles away.[22] Almost every night there were false alarms. There were persistent rumors that Germans had dropped behind American lines and were heading to the beach. In the early invasion period nervous GIs repeatedly called out in alarm, imagining German paratroopers in the dark sky.[23] Anyone stepping out of their foxhole at night had to worry about being mistaken for the enemy and getting shot.

Cortland found himself working guard duty one night. He and another soldier walked the perimeter. "That was the scariest time because you didn't know if the Germans would attack. They were still in the area. I heard this noise. The first thing I thought was [that it was] a German sniper. So, I dropped into a ditch."[24] Corty peered out from the ground and was relieved to see it was only a dog, a St. Bernard.

The German Army was renowned for its strong counterattacks, and a retaliation was expected. Utah Beach was isolated from the other Allied landing sites. If there were serious trouble, they would be on their own. If the Germans did force back the invasion, then the 1st Engineer Special Brigade and its attached troops would have to oversee the American retreat to England. Cortland and the 519th men would be among the last to leave and likely killed or captured. The dreaded German counterattack never materialized, but the anxiety felt on the beach persisted until the end of July. On the 25th a massive American air bombardment broke the German positions. American forces surged forward, pushing the enemy far from the beaches and toward Paris. The sudden advance silenced the German artillery, finally allowing the men at Utah Beach to work in relative safety.

9
BEACH WORK

The men of the 519th Port Battalion worked Utah Beach for five months.[1] They were charged with the crucial task of unloading supplies from the ships, supporting the offensive against the Germans. In 1944–45 *The Stars and Stripes* published a pocket-sized Transportation Corps history booklet. It proclaimed the port battalions' task with exuberance:

> Without the loads from the ships there would have been no "battle of the beaches." Battles depend on ammunition; food; and POL—petrol, oil, lubricants. The men of the port battalions, DUKW units and harbor craft gangs knew this as they shoved off early on June 6.
>
> Behind the invasion headlines lay the "miracle" of the Normandy beaches. Miracle? No! Just blood and sweat. No miracle to the port battalion men who unloaded tons upon tons of material for the D-Day buildup! No miracle to that single battalion which worked 102 straight days and nights without time off! No miracle to another, which in a single night unloaded 1226 tons of hellish cargo![2]

The most useful Atlantic seaports were not yet open to the Allies. Until July 1944 nearly all supplies had to come through the Normandy beaches. The 1st ESB headquarters landed on D-Day, taking command of the beach the next morning, June 7th. Its combat engineers raced to clear obstacles and wreckage from the beach. They drained

Supplies pour ashore on a Normandy Beach, June 6, 1944. Barrage balloons float overhead to protect the ships from low-flying enemy strafers. This photo was taken by a Coast Guard combat photographer. (USNA)

expansive inundated areas, reclaiming land that had been flooded as part of the German defenses. All core 1st ESB units were trained in the detection and clearance of mines, which sped the opening of the planned supply dump areas. Dump management units were able to check and clear their areas without having to wait for help from the engineers. Beach dumps were ready to receive supplies by the end of June 7th.[4]

519th Port Battalion Headquarters transported to the beach in a landing craft, June 7, 1944. Captain Samuel Klauber appears at left. Note the helmet of the 90th Infantry Division soldier at the bottom right. (DHW)

Joining the 519th under the command of the 1st Engineer Special Brigade were two other port battalions, the 490th and the 518th. Apart from its white officers, the 490th Port Battalion was an all-African-American unit. The port companies' first duty was to unload the ships that had brought them from England. Once this was accomplished the men were transported to shore. Various units of the 519th Port Battalion hit the beach on June 7th, 8th, 9th, and 10th.[5] They dropped off their bags and immediately returned to the anchored supply ships to continue unloading.

There were special logistical challenges in the first few days requiring much improvisation. Unloading ships by sea was an unusual operation for the men trained to work in ports. Hundreds of supply ships waited in an area roughly four miles long and five miles wide. Each ship was supposed to arrive with all the necessary cargo nets, hooks, cables, slings, and various other gear needed for discharge. However, some American vessels arriving in the first wave lacked these important items. Port companies arrived in France without their own stevedoring equipment. As an interim solution, the men borrowed gear from the UK ships.[6] The shortage was solved only after the 519th established a gear shop on the beach to produce their own slings and cables using whatever material they had on hand.[7] In the first few weeks information from newly arriving ships was not communicated well. Rather than waiting for a specific assignment, port company crews were often sent out to unload whatever ship they happened upon.[8] The workers found that the ships' cargo had been loaded to capacity. This was not accommodating to the speedy unloading desired for the opening days of the invasion. Invasion planners had devised a breakwater made from intentionally sunk Liberty Ships. The 1st ESB's "Gooseberry" was supposed to provide a sheltered artificial harbor, but it ended up being a wasted effort.[9] All these problems were resolved quickly, and the supply activity improved as the weeks progressed.

UNLOADING AT SEA

The port companies worked in twelve-hour shifts. At the beginning of his workday Cortland caught a ride in an amphibious 2½-ton truck, the Army's DUKW. This remarkable vehicle received high praise from the 1st Engineer Special Brigade:

> The DUKW (2½ ton 6x6 Amphibious Truck) is worth its weight in gold in an assault landing such as NEPTUNE; no self respecting invasion should be without them.[10]

Its ability to drive both on land and in water was invaluable during the initial D-Day landing and in the following supply operations. Pronounced "duck," this fitting acronym derived from General Motors Corporation's model naming conventions. "D" represented the design year (1942). "U" stood for "utility." "K" signified all-wheel drive. "W" indicated the vehicle employed two powered rear axles. Drivers from the 1st ESB amphibious truck companies ferried port company work sections to the supply ships. Coastal ships waited a short half-mile ride from the beach. The military's largest supply vessels, the Liberty Ships and Victory Ships, were anchored three miles from shore.

Cortland remained on the DUKW while the rest of the men climbed up the rope ladder to the ship's deck. These men opened the hatch covers, raised the ship's booms and got to work. An eight-man crew stepped down a ladder into the hold. There were two Tech/5 "headers" working as foremen along with six longshoremen with the rank of private. These headers were meant to supervise, but in actual practice everybody shared the heavy work.

The hold crew's assignment was to prepare the cargo for hoisting. Supplies had been layered in the hold so that the port company men walked directly on top of the crates, bags, bombs, etc. They lifted out material, working their way down to the bottom floor of the hold. Items on the far edges of the hold needed to be repositioned directly under the square hatch opening. This was usually done with greased rollers, a prybar, and a lot of muscle. There was no room for a forklift below decks, but some situations allowed the more distant items to be moved using pulley and cables. The crew relaxed while the winches pulled the supplies across the floor to the hatch opening.[11]

A hook from the ship's boom was lowered down to each load. The hold crew fitted a cable or rope sling through the bottom open space of the wooden pallet and fastened it around the block of supplies. There were many different specialty slings and hooks used for carrying various objects. Loose packages such as gasoline-filled jerry cans were cradled in a cargo net. Solomon Fein, a member of the neighboring 518th Port Battalion, recalled how his hold crew threw these 41-pound gas cans across the hold, which was a lot quicker than carrying them. They did the same with heavy ammunition boxes, tossing them to the feet of another man, and onto the cargo net.

A 1949 training photo showing a DUKW receiving cargo from the ship's hatch. (ATM)

A laden port battalion DUKW motoring to port at Cherbourg, France. August 18, 1944. (USNA)

When the cargo was secure a go-ahead was waved to the signalman above. A two-man winch team (ranked as Tech/4) then hoisted the load through the hatch, swung it over the edge of the ship, and lowered it into a waiting DUKW, Rhino barge, or landing craft. A Rhino barge was a large floating platform that could carry loads larger and heavier than what could be handled by a DUKW. These were typically used to transport vehicles, telephone poles, rails, timber, etc. Either in the hold or on deck one or two Tech/5 checkers cataloged everything that left for shore. A sergeant oversaw the whole operation of a hatch. This sergeant often also worked as signalman, but in an ideal situation the two positions were separated. A Liberty Ship had five hatches, each worked by a different crew.[12]

Cortland worked as a "swamper." He stood on the DUKW, moored it to the cargo ship's side, eased the cargo into place, unhooked the line, and cast off the DUKW. "We worked long hours. I think a DUKW could hold one net. We would unhook it, jump off, and get in another one. What you would do is jump from one DUKW to the next."[13] All this was done in rough waters. Dave Weaver, a winch operator, described

the dangerous work. "That was a risky job, because when that DUKW came up there was a big rope with a hook on it, and they would hook that into the DUKW, and then they'd kind of pull against it and run their motor a little bit hard, and crank the rudder so they would hold to the ship. But all at the same time it was fairly tough. They were bobbing up and down. The sergeant in charge was usually the signalman, and he'd be looking over the edge, and holding his hand up. When he dropped his hand you dropped the load in. Well, sometimes there was a little time gap where you'd hit it pretty hard in the DUKW. Sometimes that thing would be swinging when it went over the edge!"[14]

Pvt. Alfred Roberts and Pvt. Louis Peters load their DUKW with ammunition from a Liberty Ship off the coast of France. August 18, 1944. (USNA)

The DUKW drivers were constantly gunning their motors to keep in position. The ponderous cargo net swung back and forth, dropping suddenly. It would be easy for a guy with Corty's job to get knocked into the water. The recommended weight loaded into a DUKW was almost three tons. In the urgency of the first week, however, the load was allowed to be even greater—a weight just short of sinking the craft.[15] Corty couldn't help but imagine what would happen if his

77

1958 training photo showing a wheeled crane from Fort Eustis Motorpool shifting cargo from a DUKW to a 2-½ ton truck. (ATM)

DUKW was hit by the Germans while he was working. "I didn't mind moving the ammo. It was the gas that worried me. I didn't want to burn to death."[16]

Loaded DUKWs motored back to shore, met with the Beach Dispatch, and were directed to supply dumps in fields two miles inland. Wherever possible narrow beach roads were made one-way to avoid traffic congestion. As soon as the Germans retreated, new supply dumps were established six or seven miles from shore. The original beach dumps continued to be maintained, primarily for the 1st Engineer Brigade's own operational needs. Driving to dumps miles from shore was wearing on the DUKWs, and it took time away from their service on the water.

In the weeks following D-Day, more unloading equipment arrived, allowing the DUKWs to deliver their cargo at five transfer points only half a mile from the water's edge. Here GMC Jimmy 2½-ton trucks received the supplies and drove to the inland supply dumps. The dumps were all categorized by supply type. A DUKW or truck was supposed to be loaded with cargo of only one type so it would not need to visit more than one supply dump before returning to the beach. Cranes at the supply dumps transferred the material to trucks, which drove off immediately to the front lines.[17] By the end of August an express trucking route was organized in France with the starting point at Utah Beach's supply dumps. This was the famed Red Ball Express.[18]

Meeting the Allies' immediate supply needs required a little recklessness. Weight restrictions on ship booms (loading arms) were willfully ignored. Port soldiers risked injury when they snapped. More than one hastily loaded and unbalanced barge capsized. Worn-out DUKWs could not spare the time for repair. The 1st Engineer Special Brigade men worked them until they busted. Rhino barges broke in half. Storage space was limited, so gasoline, ammunition, and equipment were soon piled on the roadsides and around villages.[19]

THE STORM

A severe storm hit Normandy beach on June 19–22. Cortland remarked, "It got so bad that the Coast Guard chased us off the water."[20]

It was a major disruption to the supply work, but offered the men a chance to rest, albeit in soggy foxholes. The storm came on so suddenly that John Shireman and his work section were left stranded on a ship, unable to return to shore. After several days they ran out of food. The Merchant Marine would not send help in the choppy waters. It was African-American soldiers from a DUKW company who came to the rescue. "They kept us alive. Guys came out in DUKWs, and hooked on rations on ropes we'd throw overboard. That's almost irresponsible to come out in a storm like that, but we were stranded out there. We had no way to get in, and we had nothing to eat. The storm was raging. The waves were so high that the guys came almost halfway up the ship, when they were bobbing beside. They were taking a terrific chance. If they hit the ship they could capsize. I give them all the credit they deserve. They were a good group."[21]

The Stars and Stripes' Transportation Corps booklet gave a rousing description of that June storm:

> The weather was rotten all through June. On June 20 all hell broke loose in the channel. For three days while a storm raged the Allied supply line was knocked into a cocked hat. The DUKWs got off the waves. Heading out from the beaches, the piers wove

Beached coastal ships on Utah Beach. (BCK)

and then buckled like accordions. Ships floundered. Derelict craft jammed the beaches. Vessels were pounded to pieces and capsized. Giant causeways, which had been towed across the channel in sections, were twisted beyond repair. When it was over our men had as big a mess to clean up as they had in the early days after D-Day. The artificial harbor installations were wrecked, the sands were strewn with debris of smashed barges, landing craft and vehicles. But the men pitched in, and within a few days things were shipshape again.[22]

As soon as the weather cleared, the men returned to their supply work. The US Navy's LST (Landing Ship, Tank) was specifically designed to hit the beach and discharge its tanks, trucks, and troops directly on solid ground. The Beach Operations Section on Utah Beach wanted to employ a similar technique with the relatively larger coastal ships. Beaching would put great stress on the ship's hull, but it would speed up the unloading process.

After some initial reluctance from the Navy, General Omar Bradley authorized the practice on June 20. The risk to the ships was necessary to address the work-time lost during the storm. A ship was brought in close to shore at high tide. As the tide went out, the vessel slowly lowered into the sand. Trucks and DUKWs could then drive up to the beached ship until the rising tide floated it back up hours later. This unconventional approach reduced unloading time, but it was limited by ship size and constrained beach space. The gigantic Liberty and Victory ships and the majority of coastal ships needed to remain anchored in deep water.[23]

Increasing logistical strain was being placed on the Utah and Omaha beaches. Allied invasion planners had anticipated capturing the French port of Cherbourg by June 14. This would allow shipping directly from the United States. However, the German defense was stronger than anticipated. The Americans finally took Cherbourg on June 27, but they found the port unusable. The Germans had demolished dock equipment and sunk over 100 vessels and tons of debris to block the port's waterways. There would be a month of clean-up before Cherbourg could handle a sufficient shipping.

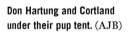

Alex Wanczak resting on some jerry cans. (GW)

Don Hartung and Cortland under their pup tent. (AJB)

Some of Cortland's friends: Richard C. Krause, William J. Kelly, and Dominic C. Parise. (AJB)

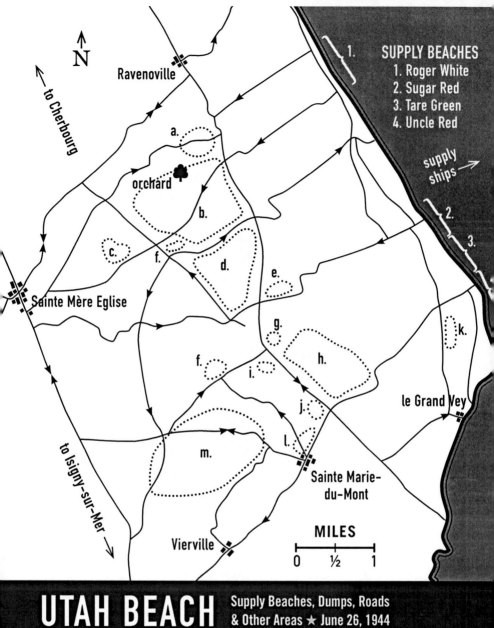

UTAH BEACH
Supply Beaches, Dumps, Roads
& Other Areas ★ June 26, 1944

SUPPLY BEACHES
1. Roger White
2. Sugar Red
3. Tare Green
4. Uncle Red

- **a. Class III:** petroleum
- **b. Transit Area "B":** an assembly point for incoming troops
- **c. Class X:** non-military (civilian aid)
- **d. Class V:** ammunition
- **e. Chemical Warfare:** decontamination and smoke screen (both unused)
- **f. Class II:** clothing, individual equipment, etc. and **Class IV:** construction materials
- **g. Signal:** radio and telephone
- **h. Class III:** petroleum
- **i. Class I:** food and water
- **j. Medical**
- **k. Naval**
- **l. Engineer Service:** de-mining, road maintenance, construction, etc.
- **m. Transit Area "A":** deemed undesirable location. Closed on D-Day +14.

Meanwhile, other potentially useful French ports remained under firm enemy control. These obstinate German garrisons would not surrender until September. Denied a working seaport, the Allies' supply needs in the summer of 1944 would rely almost completely on Normandy's beaches.[24] From July 1st to the 25th 447,000 tons landed in France with 392,000 of that (88%) flowing over the beaches.[25] From June to the end of beach operations in mid-November, 726,014 tons passed through Utah Beach.[26] The 519th Port Battalion unloaded 290,593 tons of this.[27] One out of every four loads was a petroleum product, mostly gasoline. This was perhaps the most crucial supply type. The advancing 1st and 3rd Armies had a desperate need for gas. They burned through 400,000 gallons every day. American Sherman tanks ran only one or two miles per gallon during combat.[28] In addition to moving supplies the 1st Engineer Special Brigade was responsible for managing 801,000 incoming troops and 163,529 vehicles.[29]

IN THE APPLE ORCHARD

On June 24th the battalion left the beach, moving north and inland to an apple orchard located one-and-a-half miles south of the French town of Ravenoville. The 279th Port Company remained in foxholes near the beach. Headquarters moved briefly to a farmhouse, and then returned to the beach on June 27th. They set up their command in a concrete German bunker overlooking the water.[30] Under the apple trees the port companies made more substantial shelters built of abandoned enemy material, salvaged wood, and debris. Cortland explained, "We used dunnage. It was the wood used in cargo ships to pack the supplies. They threw it away when they were done with it."[31] Although rustic, the new accommodations were far more comfortable than the sandy holes on the beach.

John Shireman described the evenings in the orchard. "When we'd get back on shore we'd get a pretty good meal at night as a rule. But it was all tent life, and we burrowed in the ground and kind of made little huts. The guys would all get out at night and talk for a little bit and have some coffee. We'd get some cans and cut a hole in the top, pour water in, and boil coffee in there. We'd do things like that until bedtime, then we'd go to our tents."[32]

519th Port Battalion HQ housed in a German bunker on Utah Beach. Dallas Rudrud, Bruce Kramlich, and Sgt. Rydski (spelling?). (BCK)

The Duchemin family, owners of the apple orchard. (BCK)

Normandy's apple orchards were cultivated to pro- The 519th Port duce Calvados, an apple brandy. This particular farm Battalion's orchard was owned by the Duchemin family. They were only camp south of Ravenoville. (BCK) too pleased to share the product with the American liberators. Some guys were known to carry Calvados in their canteens instead of water. Cortland remembered with a chuckle, "At night the guys were all getting drunk, and the CO couldn't figure out how."[33] Their camp was far from town shops, and the battalion officers living back at the beach didn't know all those apples were destined for the Duchemin distillery.

One drawback to living in the apple orchard was its distance to the beach. The men had to start walking an hour before the start of their shift and walk back another hour after a tiring twelve hours at work. It was especially aggravating to watch truckloads of German POWs chauffeured to their light duties on the beach. Thousands of these prisoners of war were used for manual labor on the beach, in supply dumps, and on the roads. Eventually a motor pool was set up for the 519th Port Battalion and rides were provided to the exhausted GIs.[34]

Above: Matt Marvin and another GI with the Duchemin children. (BCK)
Below: Hut interior belonging to Dave Weaver and Harold Chitty. (DHW)

IN PROUD MEMORY
OF OUR DEAD

1ST ENGINEER
SPECIAL BRIGADE

H.HOUR 0630
D DAY 6 JUNE 1944

KEEP OFF
THESE

On October 18, 1944 Irving Sugarman wrote a letter to his wife. His concise description evokes the mood of those soldiers working on Utah Beach:

> Ask him to imagine himself in little hole in the sand with sand in his clothes, on his body, in his eyes, nose, mouth, ears, with rain coming down making it mud—cold! Trying to sleep after hours and hours of work, with Heinies [German fighter planes] flying around and the guns crashing, so that you nearly jump out of your skin while the Heinies drop flares that light up the area like daylight, and you feel as big as a house and seems as though all they can see is you. Then you hear that whining roar and you shake all over and pray and think to yourself, "He's coming straight at me," and the roar grows louder, and the machine guns crackle away, and if you've got the strength to turn your head where you're trying to burrow into the ground, you can see the tracers and the ack ack bursting almost like a solid curtain of red and white fire.[35]

> Then you hear that awful whistle and it grows louder then a thrrrump and another one, and another one, and the sand caves in from the concussion, and the air is sucked out of your lungs. After what seems like hours, they finally leave, and when you find you're still in one piece, you dig yourself out of the sand and grab your trench shovel and run around in the dark to see if there's anyone to dig out.

> Then blessed daylight, and you go into drizzle that soaks you to the bones and work, another long day, and you have the same thing to look forward to at night—another sleepless horrible night, and you don't know if you're going to wake up the next morning.[36]

Monument to the 1st Engineer Special Brigade inaugurated on the one-year anniversary of D-Day, June 6, 1945. The structure was built on top of a concrete German bunker at Utah Beach. All 1st ESB and attached units are listed on the monument's sides. (AJB)

The 519th drives through
a ruined French town on
its way to the train station.
(AJB)

10

TO ANTWERP

The use of the Normandy beaches continued longer than had been planned. The French port of Cherbourg was captured in late June but required extensive reconstruction before it could be used. There was delay in capturing other French ports, which led to a backlog of Allied shipping. The great Belgian port of Antwerp offered the solution to this supply bottleneck.

By late August of 1944 the Allies were pushing back the Germans through France to the east side of the River Seine. The Allied command was pleased with this unexpectedly rapid advance, yet the success posed a severe logistical problem. As the fighting moved east and north, the supply dumps at Normandy and Cherbourg became more distant. With no large port close enough to the front lines, supplies had to be sent by truck. Red Ball Express drivers moved truckloads of crucial supplies a distance of 300 miles or more. The limited production of tractor-trailers necessitated the use of relatively small trucks. Gasoline, ammunition, and food all had to be carried in the 2½-ton GMC Jimmy. The Quartermaster Trucking companies were performing impressively, yet this method of supply was far from ideal. The Allies wanted Antwerp. This Belgian city held Europe's largest seaport, and it was well-situated to quickly supply the army.

News of the approaching Allies encouraged a hasty German retreat from the city. Defying German gunshots, four Belgians climbed to the top of the cathedral spire to rip down a giant Nazi flag. As they raised the Belgian flag in its place a crowd cheered below. While the Germans withdrew, they set explosives to destroy the port's warehouses, cranes, and unloading equipment. The Belgian resistance scoured the docks thoroughly, defusing the bombs. Thanks to their efforts, the arriving Allies found the port facilities largely intact. Amid ecstatic cheers, Antwerp was liberated by British-Canadian forces on September 4, 1944, yet the port could not receive Allied shipping.[1] Entrenched German troops still controlled the waterway leading to the sea.

BATTLE OF THE SCHELDT

To make Antwerp's port usable the enemy needed to be removed from the Scheldt River estuary. However, Field Marshal Montgomery preferred a more daring scheme that would make Antwerp unnecessary. Operation Market Garden called for British and American paratroopers to secure a series of bridges over the main rivers of the German-held Netherlands. Success would open a highway straight into Germany, with the hope of ending the war by Christmas. Regrettably, the complicated plan failed.

Attention was immediately brought back to opening the port. On October 2nd the Canadian First Army began their assault. South Beveland, the peninsula at the mouth of the Scheldt River, and Walcheren Island were defended by the very determined German Fifteenth Army. Thousands lost their lives in this flooded rainy landscape north of Antwerp. After a month of vicious fighting the Germans had surrendered their claim to the river. By November 8, 1944, 12,873 Canadian, British, and Polish troops were killed, wounded, or missing. Nearly half of these casualties were Canadians. If one also includes the September fighting leading up to the battle, then the total number swells to about 15,000. While most of the German defenders managed to escape, 41,043 were taken prisoner, and tens of thousands were killed or wounded. The grueling Battle of the Scheldt was successful in dislodging the Germans, allowing the port to open. With the surrounding banks secured, the British Royal Navy began what would be two weeks of sweeping mines from the harbors.[2]

304th Port Company men posing in front of their train. Mike DeLaura appears at the lower left in a knit cap. The French conductor appears in the back with the black hat. (AMD)

40 & 8s

The arrival of November's winter weather made the Normandy beaches completely unsuitable for unloading operations. Beach activity declined as the Allies prepared for the opening of Antwerp's port. The core units of the 1st Engineer Special Brigade were separated into engineer combat battalions and sent to the Netherlands to join the US Ninth Army.[3] The 279th Port Company was released from the 519th and trucked off to the port at Le Havre, France. The 518th Port Battalion moved on to port operations in Gent, Belgium. On November 14th the men of the 519th were loaded on trucks and DUKWs and were driven to Chef-du-Pont. On the 15th another company, the 281st Port Company, joined the 519th as they boarded trains for Antwerp.[4]

Cortland and the others were loaded onto "40 & 8s." These WWI-era French railway cars were originally designed to hold forty men or eight horses. This may sound spacious, but the GIs were cramped and uncomfortable. Corty recalled, "You were lucky to find a place to sit down. We slept sitting down, or leaning against something. We didn't get too much sleep."[5] Ray Sonoski of the 304th Port Company

described the trip. "Oh boy, that was something else! We were in small boxcars. I don't know how many of us were in there, but I'll tell you this much: It was very cramped. We had our equipment, rifles, full field pack, helmets, and whatever. There were no facilities, and we were lucky to find a corner to sit down. Those were the comforts of the train."[6]

James Dolan (bottom left), 2nd Lt. Gardner (bottom right), Herb Koller (above Dolan), Don Hartung (far right). (AJB)

The slow-moving train rarely stopped, but at one French town Corty was treated to a simple pleasure: "We stopped once for coffee. I lost my canteen, so I had to drink mine out of an old juice can. I remember that very well."[7] Dave Weaver commented further on the journey. "My most vivid memory of our train trip to Antwerp: When stopped en route in French villages and towns people offered us (for money) bottles of water. When stopped en route in Belgium we were offered gratis fruit and wine! This formed my lifelong opinion of the citizenry of the two countries!"[8]

In Belgium their train stopped to allow an express train through. It was carrying wounded from the front lines. Cortland and the others got out and started talking with some locals, who offered beer to the

GIs. "They just handed it to us. They were happy to see us!"[9] At least once the train came to a halt near a restaurant or café, allowing the men to buy some good food. Apart from that it was C-rations and K-rations for meals. There were no toilets in the train cars, so the guys had to go find a tree. The train's whistle announced that it was starting up again. If somebody didn't make it back on the train, he might hop on a truck to the next town, and get back on the train from there.[10] The unpleasant ride went on for five days. In the evening of November 18, 1944 the battalion arrived in Antwerp.[11]

John Shireman (top middle with cracker), Dave Weaver (top far right), Harold Chitty (between Shireman and Weaver). (AJB)

A V-1 above Antwerp. (AJB)

11
THE V-WEAPONS

As the Allied forces pushed the enemy back to Germany, waves of support troops followed into Belgium. These thousands of American, British, Canadian, and Polish troops needed immediate housing. Recently liberated Belgian towns agreed to provide the requisite buildings. The Belgian national government would later reimburse the towns, considering this cost to be part of its contribution to the war effort.[1] In Antwerp the 519th Port Battalion was provided with an apartment building on the docks. Tampico Flats stood in the Luchtbal neighborhood in the north of the city, close to the Netherlands border.

When Cortland first learned of their new living quarters he was genuinely excited. Having lived in a hole in the ground for nearly four months he and the guys were looking forward to better accommodations. "The first thing I thought was, 'Showers!' But, when we got there we saw there were none. I guess we all smelled the same, so no one knew the difference. There was one bathroom at the end of the hall for fifteen guys. There were two of us in a room with a bunk bed. There were no mattresses, so we had to put straw on the bunks. And there were no windows—we pretty near froze to death. You'd lay your wet socks out at night and they'd still be wet the next day."[2]

ANTWERP UNDER SIEGE
There were dangers in Antwerp beyond the mere cold. The windows in Cortland's room had been shattered by explosions. German fighter

Captured German V-1 (above) and V-2 (below) on display
in Antwerp's 1945 Groenplaats Exposition. (TDD)

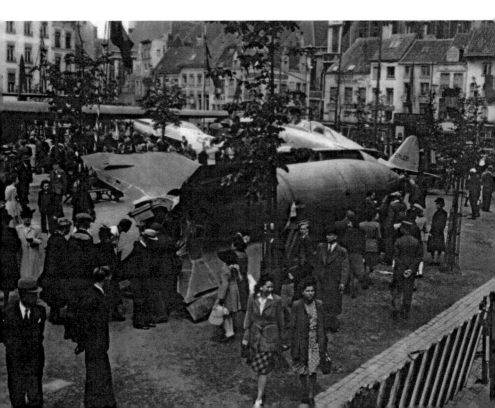

planes would occasionally bomb and strafe the port, but the greatest apprehension was caused by the Germans' startling V-weapons. The V-1 and the V-2 were the earliest cruise and ballistic missiles, respectively. The V-1's engine featured a distinctive banging and buzzing noise. This characteristic earned it the name "buzz bomb." Flying straight and relatively low, its timing device cut the engine, causing the rocket to glide down to earth and explode.

The V-2 was launched at a higher trajectory. Rising sixty to seventy miles above the city it then dropped down silently, plummeting faster than the speed of sound. As revenge for the Allied bombings of German cities, Hitler chose London's civilian population as the primary target. The V-weapons hitting London were launched from the French coast. After Allied troops overran these sites, the retreating Germans turned their attack on the port of Antwerp.

On October 7, 1944 the first V-2 exploded in the city. The first V-1 followed four days later. On October 13th the grave risk to the citizenry was made apparent. A V-2 hit Schilderstraat that morning killing thirty and injuring forty-five. Almost six thousand V-1s and V-2s would rain down on Antwerp during the 175-day bombardment. Antwerp and its suburbs witnessed tragedy nearly every day.

The deadliest V-weapon attack of the war coincided with the opening of the German's Ardennes Offensive on December 16, 1944. A V-2 missile dropped directly on the packed Rex Cinema. 567 military men and civilians were killed in that single attack. 291 people were injured, and eleven buildings were destroyed.[3] Men of the 304th Port Company had often visited this theater. John Shireman reflected, "That was the night I didn't go. I was staying home and writing letters."[4] Cortland explained that all theaters were then closed and large gatherings prohibited. "After that they ordered us—there were no crowds allowed."[5]

Ray Sonoski recalled the V-1 rockets hitting near Tampico Flats. "It was nerve wracking of course. We had them all the time. The buzz bombs would come over and then crash maybe a mile down the road. The V-2s, of course, it was something else because you didn't see them at all. They just dropped out of the sky on top of you and that was it."[6] Cortland remembered the noisy V-1s. "As long as you could hear them you knew you were OK. It was when the sound stopped that you had to hit the ground. We were always under attack by buzz bombs. Once we even had to leave the church service which was held in a tent."[7]

A member of headquarters, Larry Botzon, described how the 519th men gradually became desensitized to the threat. "If I recall correctly I was on the top floor and the first couple of nights when we heard the buzz bombs coming we ran down to the first floor, or maybe it was the basement. After it passed we would go back up. After a short while one became what could be called a fatalist, that is, if you are going to be hit—you are going to be hit. Therefore we, or at least I, just stayed in my bunk and prayed it would pass us by."[8]

Injuries to men in the battalion were common. Multiple men from the 519th received the Purple Heart for wounds received during the German bombardment. Cuts from flying glass were the most typical injuries.[9] Indeed, by the end of the war nearly all the windows in the entire port area had been blown out by exploding V-weapons.[10] The randomness and suddenness of the attacks was unnerving, but everyone tried to put it out of their minds. Newcomers did not handle the anxiety so well. A March 26, 1945 article in *TIME* magazine relates the story of some combat troops sent to Antwerp for rest and relaxation. After one day they pleaded to be sent back to the front lines.[11]

CLOSE CALLS

In early January Cortland was out walking when he heard that familiar buzzing in the sky above. The noise of the rocket grew louder, then silence. He dove to the ground just as the rocket exploded nearby. One of the bomb fragments slammed into the ground beside him. "The thing flew right over my head!" Corty picked up the crumpled slab of aluminum as a souvenir. He later showed it to some friends, recounting the near miss. One of these guys was an MP. "He told me I could give it to him and one of the prisoners could make something nice out of it." The MP kept watch over German POWs. Apparently one of these prisoners had been a metal worker in civilian life. For a small

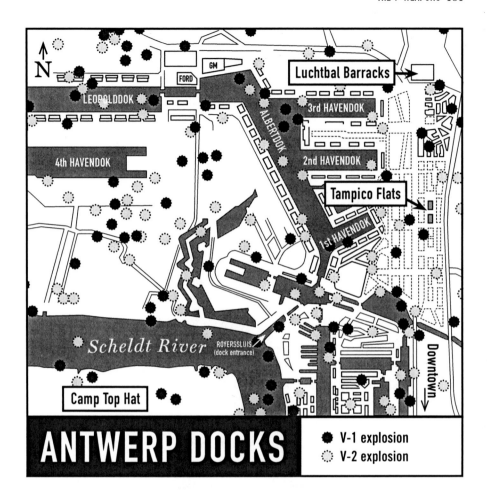

ANTWERP DOCKS

- ● V-1 explosion
- ○ V-2 explosion

Cortland's bracelet made from V-1 shrapnel. (AJB)

price Corty had an interesting keepsake made for his girlfriend. The prisoner fashioned the rough shrapnel into a charming heart-shaped bracelet. "I gave him three packs of cigarettes. He almost kissed me!"[12]

The heart and band were decorated with a floral folk art motif. The face of the heart was engraved with the text, "MARGE FROM CORTY." An inscription on the back notes the place, "Antwerp" and "January 5, 1945." Cortland scratched in the source of the shrapnel himself, "V1." Rather than mailing it home, Corty kept the bracelet with him to present to his girlfriend in person.[13] John Shireman's own close call with a V-bomb resulted in a similar gift for his sweetheart. "On guard duty I was blown against a warehouse. I had a bracelet made from the shrapnel."[14] His simple wristband was made by an American soldier. Bruce Kramlich also left Antwerp with a V-1 bracelet. It must have been a common souvenir for the Army port workers.

The V-weapon attacks on Antwerp ended in late March 1945 as the German launch positions in Germany and the Netherlands were overrun by advancing Allied troops. Between October 7, 1944 and March 30, 1945 there was only one day, March 17, when a rocket did not hit the city. The Germans hurled their V-weapons into the Allied supply center night and day. The port area was hit by 150 V-1s and 152 V-2s. Fifty-three Allied military men were killed in the docks, along with 131 Belgian civilian workers. 174 troops and 380 civilians were severely injured. Two warehouses were destroyed. One of these received a direct hit causing 148 casualties at once. Twenty port berths and one canal lock were damaged. 150 ships were sunk or damaged.[15] The bombardment forced the Allies to redirect ammunition ships to the more distant Belgian port of Gent to protect that highly explosive cargo. Although Antwerp's docks were the intended target, inaccurate V-weapons exploded throughout the city. Greater Antwerp, its suburban neighborhoods, and adjacent areas were hit by 4,248 V-1s and 1,712 V-2s. A total of 3,752 residents were killed, with 6,074 wounded. 731 American and British servicemen were killed, and 1192 were wounded.[16]

Ruined Antwerp streets
photographed by Cortland.
(AJB)

CITY DEFENSES

Far more people would have died were it not for the defense provided by Anti-Flying Bomb Commando Antwerp X. As early as October 1944 antiaircraft artillery were deployed in an arc ten miles from the southeastern edge of the port area. Positions would shift over the months to counter the changing V-1 firing positions. Working in bone-chilling cold three brigades composed of American, British, and Polish antiaircraft batteries brought down 2,183 V-1s. What started in the fall as an 11,500-man force swelled by March to 22,000 men firing over 500 antiaircraft guns. At the end of the German bombardment Antwerp X was hitting a very high percentage of incoming V-1 rockets.[17]

During a six-day span in March 1945 the gunners stopped 89 of 91 rockets. This accomplishment is made more impressive when one considers that the V-1 offered a target smaller than any fighter plane. Constructed of steel and flying at 450 miles per hour, it was one of the fastest and best protected craft in the sky. While 648 of the targeted V-1s were destroyed in the air, 1,535 of the disabled rockets came hurtling down to the ground. Thirty men were killed and 298 were wounded.[18] The 184th AAA Gun Battalion distributed a small unit history book to its members at the end of the war. A passage relays the anxiety felt after scoring a hit:

> Shooting at Buzz Bombs was a skill that required steady nerves. As each gun fired no one knew whether the round that was on the way would bring the bomb screaming down on top of them.... It was a relief to all to see the Buzz Bomb explode in the air with a tremendous sheet of flame and cloud of smoke, followed by a mighty report. The cry of "It's coming down" saw many faces turned skyward watching the bomb. Sometimes on being hit in a vital spot, a Buzz Bomb would nose over and head straight down, screaming as it dove towards the ground, landing with a shattering explosion, the concussion of which smashed nearby buildings as though they were of cardboard. Sometimes with their motors off, the bombs would glide on their path until they crashed. Other times when hit, the V-1s would go into wild gyrations turning on their backs, climbing, turning completely around or veering off to another course. When the order "Fire"

came to the gun crews no one knew what would happen to that bomb, and the "Sweating" would begin until it crashed or went safely overhead.[19]

The Americans' P-61 Black Widow night fighter was fast enough to approach a V-1, yet bringing down the rocket from the air was still difficult. The Allies found it more effective to use their air power to disrupt German railroads supplying V-weapon launch sites. Against the supersonic V-2, there was no protection. Fortunately for the people of Antwerp, production of the V-2 was time-consuming and intensive, resulting in a rate of fire far less than that of the V-1.[20]

Allied antiaircraft artillery on display in Antwerp's 1945 Groenplaats Exposition. (AJB)

Downtown Antwerp
photographed by
Cortland. (AJB)

12

WORK IN THE PORT

Upon Antwerp's liberation the British took control of the port, placing an officer of the Royal Navy in overall command. The Americans and British were assigned separate sectors from which to move their own supplies.[1] Heading the American area was the 13th Major Port Group. Further assistance would come with the arrival of the 5th Major Port Group. The American port commander was Colonel Doswell Gullatt. Accomplished in port operations, he had commanded the 5th Engineer Special Brigade at Omaha Beach. In peacetime Europe's greatest seaport was able to move 80,000 to 100,000 tons of cargo per day. The Allies set daily goals for themselves considered to be conservative. The British were to unload 17,000 tons per day, and the industrious American Army was meant to move 22,500 tons. However, war conditions would make the port far less reliable than predicted.[2]

When the 519th Port Battalion first arrived in Antwerp the port had yet to reopen to shipping. Vessels sunk by the Germans and mines still blocked the waterways. While the British Navy cleared shipping lanes, the port soldiers spent their first four days in Antwerp cleaning their barracks and readying equipment. On November 22nd the men took part in various fatigue duties and guard detail. After a week of waiting for the estuary to be opened the first Liberty ships arrived on November 30, 1944. The Allies' urgent supply work could begin.[3]

The 519th was assigned control of two docking areas just to the west of Tampico Flats. For the duration of the war four companies were engaged in dock operations there. The 280th, 281st, 302nd, and 305th port companies discharged cargo, managed warehousing, and operated cranes, chisels, and tractors. The physical exertion on the docks earned these men a supplemental ration of sandwiches and coffee. Extra food was always welcome, and the men needed the additional calories. Cargo was driven by trucks and tractors from shipside to immense warehouses. From here port company men sorted the supplies, ordered transport, and loaded trucks and railway cars. Some material moved out of the city by canal barge.[4] Supplies from Antwerp fed the American First, Third, and Ninth armies. British port workers maintained the northern push of the Canadian First Army and British Second Army.

The Quartermaster Truck companies clearing the port were the same men who worked the Red Ball Express off Utah Beach. Now in Belgium, they drove trucks pulling 10-ton trailers. Their route, called the ABC Express Line (American-British-Canadian or Antwerp-Brussels-

Cortland at an Antwerp truck lot. (AJB)

Charleroi), was the longest express line driven in World War II. It was in use from November 30, 1944 to March 26, 1945. Trucks assembled in surge pools on the north edge of the city. They drove in caravans from Antwerp to depots at Mons, Charleroi, and Liège to supply the American First and Ninth armies. The trucks dropped off their trailers, then picked up new trailers full of materials for their return to Antwerp. Two of the truck companies drove directly into the port area to pick up supplies shipside.[5]

The US Army Transportation Corps favored railroads as the most efficient method of moving supplies. American rail freight out of Antwerp was managed by the Army's 708th Railway Grand Division. Receiving supplies at Antwerp's north railyards, their main destinations were the supply dumps east to Liège via the Antwerp-Louvain-Liège line and south to Luxembourg City via the Antwerp-Brussels-Namurluxembourg line. The British ran their own separate train routes.[6] While other 519th port companies supervised the loading of railcars, the 304th Port Company men accompanied the trains as guards.

A major responsibility of the 519th was the supervision of civilian labor. The Belgian dock workers knew their trade, but were unnerved by the random V-weapon explosions. At least one port company man was inserted into every civilian work team. The January 1945 Historical Report for the 519th Port Battalion emphasizes the benefit of pairing the civilians with soldiers who were accustomed to working under battle conditions in Normandy:

> "The coolness and devotion to duty evidenced by military personnel under adverse conditions, has produced a steadying influence on the civilian workers to the end, that stoppages or slow downs in operations due to enemy activity is held to a minimum."[7]

By March of 1945 the American and British armies had hired a total of around 20,000 Belgian civilians to move Allied supplies through Antwerp.[8] Roughly 9,000 civilians were working the docks and warehouses on any given day.[9] This freed military men for other duties, and it helped address Belgium's vast unemployment problem.[10] The

Belgian longshoremen were paid well, receiving 130 francs a day, one meal, and 30 francs "shiver money." This salary bonus was needed to encourage civilians to work in the high-risk war zone.[11] One assumes it was named for the "shivers" workers felt under the threat of V-weapons.

The Allied command was very satisfied with the effectiveness of their civilian workforce. There was, however, a strike in January, 1945. The entire 519th Port Battalion was poised to take over the dockmen's responsibilities, but only a few guard details were needed to fill in while the negotiations progressed. The Belgians returned to work after receiving guarantees of better transportation and more courteous inspections. There was another strike in February, but this too was resolved quickly. The military port companies' increased efforts helped to reduce work stoppages.[12]

The 303rd and Cortland's 304th Port Company were devoted to guard duty full-time. Ray Sonoski described their duties. "They had to get the civilians back to work—after all it was their job. They knew how to operate the port. So, we pulled guard duty. We would police the

Belgian stevedores working a ship's hatch. (AJB)

place at night to discourage thievery. There was a lot of that going on."[13]

THE BLACK MARKET

Ensuring efficient stevedore work was not the only reason for mixing American soldiers with the Belgian longshoremen. These civilians were watched to prevent pilfering. Theft of supplies was a tremendous problem for the Allies in Europe. Belgians had been living under German occupation for four years. Severe rationing had been imposed on the civilians, while the German army stripped the country of its resources to benefit the Nazi war effort. Although individual Allied soldiers were very generous to the hungry Belgian people, the liberation as a whole did little to alleviate the problem. Antwerp's port needed to be dedicated to military supply in order to maintain the Allied push into Germany. Food donations were made, and some ships delivered civilian cargo, but these limited efforts barely met the people's basic needs. Consequently, unguarded Allied trucks, trains, warehouses, and supply dumps were frequently burglarized.[14] Dave Weaver observed how common theft was on the docks: "We used to have *huge*

Antwerp docks. (AJB)

piles of rations and sometimes you'd walk around the back and see a box, and it would be empty. And you couldn't even see how they did it. They broke into it some way and took whatever was in it."[15]

Tampico Flats, the 519th and 517th port battalions' home in Antwerp. (AJB)

At the Allies' prompting, the Belgian government made it illegal for citizens to possess Allied goods of any kind. The level of enforcement and punishment varied during the war. A citizen caught with Allied supplies in an amount limited to personal use could be fined or sentenced to a few weeks in prison. A civilian found with levels of goods obviously destined for sale on the black market might be sent to jail for fifteen to eighteen months. As losses became more of a problem in the winter of 1944 the Allied command pressured the Belgians to increase penalties.[16]

It was not merely an issue of opportunistic civilians randomly stealing military goods. Entire criminal businesses were sustained by widespread raids of military equipment and supplies. Thousands of US soldiers were away without leave in 1944 and 1945. Unscrupulous GIs and civilians formed organized gangs, stealing material for the black market.[17] Gasoline dumps were especially vulnerable. During December's Battle of the Bulge some of the Allies' motorized columns were unable to get to the fight quickly because their gasoline had been stolen.

Some absolutely astounding heists were pulled off in Belgium. In the winter of 1944–45 thirty-five tons of bacon were stolen in Liège. Sadly, the Army had intended to distribute this food to the citizens of the city. In January ten tons of American chocolate disappeared from the same city. In March sixteen tons of sugar went missing in Limburg. Even the police were not above stealing from the Army. In February 1945 British military police arrested six Antwerp policemen for possession of substantial amounts of stolen Allied goods.[18]

The port company men supervising the dockers were often reluctant to enforce the rules when they knew the goods were heading home to hungry families. Dave Weaver guarded a check point for civilian stevedores leaving the wharf. "To go home the dock workers had to come through a gate, and we'd have searches of these guys. There were huge stocks of food, and that's what we'd guard on the docks. I remember one time a guy came, and he had a metal canteen—they all did. Well, his was full of sugar. We just let him go on by."[19] Not surprisingly, the very men in charge of protecting supplies might sometimes help themselves to a bottle of alcohol or carton of cigarettes. In 1945 Dave Weaver and few other soldiers brushed off the rules to spread some holiday cheer. One of the guys was friends with a Belgian girl, a barmaid at a local pub. She invited the Americans to her family's Christmas party. Mr. DePunt, the host, owned a candy shop in town, so the GIs made sure to bring a couple big bags of American sugar as a gift.[20]

TRAIN GUARD

Cortland's primary duty in Antwerp was patrolling the docks. He was occasionally assigned to guard duty aboard supply trains headed toward the front lines. At each stop trains were vulnerable to thieves. The importance of the train security is noted in the Army's official history books of the war:

> Thefts from U.S. Army supply trains and diversions of the loot into the French black market became a serious problem during the closing months of 1944. Every stolen item represented a dual loss, first in critical shipping space, and second to the military

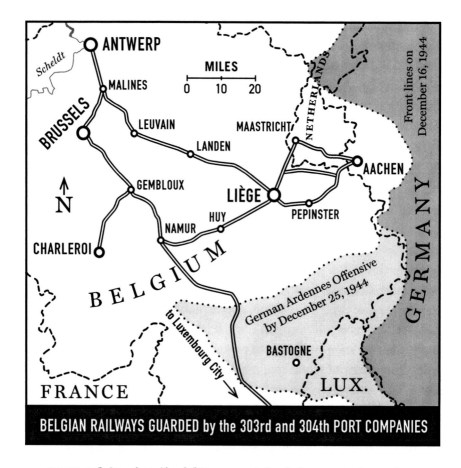

BELGIAN RAILWAYS GUARDED by the 303rd and 304th PORT COMPANIES

personnel for whom the delivery was intended. ...excessive and heavy losses caused by pilferage necessitated the detail of infantrymen and service troops as train guards.[21]

As a non-commissioned officer, a Tech/5, Cortland was in charge of a small guard team. "They would detail five of us to guard the train. We had to sit on top of the load. The gondolas [train cars] were open, so we were always wet and cold. The only thing I kept dry was my rifle. We were perfect targets for snipers. The trains were moving slow. I don't know why. I asked for a caboose [for better cover], but the guys in the train outfit were kind of mean! When we got to the terminal they'd check it [the cargo] and sign my papers that it was all there."[22]

Dave Weaver also pulled train duty. Supplies were sent to the forward depots at Liège, but also to Aachen and Brussels. "We rode in a little caboose and jumped off every time the train stopped and ran down along each side to prevent theft."[23] John Shireman shared the duty, "I don't think they spent much time trying to secure it [the supplies]. They just depended on us."[24] Much of the cargo was piled on open train cars with no security beyond a handful of port company guards.

After making a delivery Cortland and the men remained in town for several days. "We stayed in people's homes. We would meet Belgians at the terminal. They wanted to know all about America, what we did in civilian life. They were very nice people. They gave us what food they had."[25] Cortland recalled a family that had a book about the US. They were eager to hear the Americans discuss the different parts of the country pictured in their book. The Belgians were generous with food, but the Army provided field kitchens. "They had places where GIs could get something to eat. One time I got in a chow line, *waaay* in the back. This soldier up front spots me. Of course, I had the rainbow [blue arc of the ESB troops] on my helmet. He recognized it. 'Hey soldier!' he hollered. 'Do I know you?' He says, 'You were on the beach [Normandy] weren't you?' 'Yeah.' 'You belong *here*'—at the front of the line! Most of these guys in line were new from the States."[26] Corty was proud of this recognition of his work on D-Day, but perhaps more pleased that he got his meal quicker.

The train guards weren't given a specific time to return. "A couple of guys were looking up girls. I spent my time trying to find us a ride. We had to find our own way back to Antwerp. We got back the best way we could, but we didn't hurry! If there was a truck going back, we'd hitch a ride."[27] Shireman had a similar end-of-the-line experience after delivering their supplies. "Frankly, we were stranded, and had to wait for about a week before we got transportation back."[28] The Belgians were happy to take in the GIs. "We were in a house, and all of us were in a room. We got real good food, and places to stay. We had range of the area, but we couldn't get back for a week. The guys I worked with weren't very precocious [they weren't busy chasing girls], so we just kind of laid around and waited until the opportunity came to get back."[29]

Sometimes the trains carried more important cargo. "We had some sensitive stuff, locked in a car. This guy with me, he shot a guy. Somebody tried to get onboard, so he shot him. I saw someone climb up on the car. Then I saw a flash."[30] The train kept moving, and Cortland didn't see what happened to the would-be thief. He turned to his fellow guard. "I said to him, 'Give me your bullet [the spent shell].' I gave him mine. I think they gave us 5 or 6 rounds of ammo. You had to turn it in when you returned. You had to go through a lot of rigamarole, so I told them my gun misfired. I didn't want to fill out all the papers. I was always getting in trouble for little infractions anyway."[31] The port company men were authorized to shoot anyone attempting to steal from their train. Such use of force required an official report, but in this case Cortland judged the incident minor enough to avoid the hassle.

13

THE ARDENNES OFFENSIVE

In mid-December Irving Sugarman was convalescing in a hospital in Liège. A V-1 explosion outside Tampico Flats had thrown some debris against his spine. He was sent to the quieter city for surgery. Liège had also been a German target, but the V-weapon bombardment ended on November 30th.[1] In the church-turned-hospital Sugarman was relieved to have some time away from Antwerp and its daily bombs. On December 15th his rest was interrupted by the familiar sound of explosions. V-1s and V-2s began dropping around the city. He watched the German air attack through the high windows. "What a shock to see those German Fokkers [bombers] flying in the sky!"[2] The next day he learned German troops had smashed through the Allied lines. One enemy column was fast approaching Liège. Luftwaffe bombers roared over the city to bomb the railyard on the edge of town. Coincidentally, another 304th Port Company soldier was also recuperating in Liège, perhaps in the same hospital. While guarding a Liberty Ship, Ray Sonoski took a fall and broke his kneecap. Neither had fully recuperated, but both men were eager to get back to Antwerp. They did not realize that this was exactly where the Germans had planned to go.

Hitler aimed to retake Antwerp. Although his V-weapons had hampered supply movement, the great port was still feeding the Allied advance into Germany. In a highly unexpected counteroffensive, roughly 250,000 German troops poured across the snowy forests of Belgium and Luxembourg on December 16th, 1944. Coinciding with the ground offensive, a new wave of V-1 bombs flew into Antwerp from Holland. This attack came at a time when everyone thought the Germans were stuck in the defensive. Alarm spread throughout the city. Ill-prepared, the Allies scrambled to defend the port. Antiaircraft guns were moved to counter the new V-1 flight path. To safeguard their cargo from capture by the advancing Germans, supply trains ceased delivering to the front.[3] All port troops suspended supply work, took up arms, and were positioned to guard key areas.

Cortland was moved to protect a frigid trainyard in Antwerp. "During the breakthrough we had to get ammunition. They weren't expecting the Germans to attack, so they didn't have enough for us. I went to Schwartz, my supply sergeant [S/Sgt Julian Schwartzberg?], and he only gave me six rounds. 'What am I gonna do with six rounds?' I said. So, he says, 'You can shove them up your ass and pretend you're a bomb!'"[4] Obviously, the supply sergeant was frustrated with complaints about the limited ammunition. Anxious troops heard rumors of German paratroopers dressed in American uniforms. Thick fog added to the anxiety. The port command was also concerned about incursion by water. Cortland and his comrades dropped depthcharges in the canals as a precaution against German frogmen (combat swimmers).

The German army had pushed fifty miles beyond the Allied lines, but by December 23rd–26th the Americans managed to halt the breakthrough. Clear weather allowed Allied air power to join the action. By then the Germans had outrun their supply lines, and Patton's Third Army had arrived from the south of France. The enemy retreated slowly, and the Allies pursued them. When April brought the end of the V-bombs, there was little excitement for Cortland and the 519th. "Nothing really interesting happened, not on my shift anyway."[5] Cargo moved smoothly from ships to trucks, trains, and barges. It was carried to supply dumps, and joined the combat troops for their final push into Germany.

14

WAR'S END

There was a startling announcement on April 12, 1945—Franklin D. Roosevelt had died. A somber 519th Port Battalion organized a memorial service on the parade field. A month later the news in Antwerp would be joyous. Germany finally surrendered to the Allies on May 7, 1945, ending the war in Europe. The US Army rapidly moved to demobilize. A military presence would remain to support a crippled Europe, but the bulk of Americans could withdraw. The most seasoned troops were eligible to go home to the US. Most were apprehensive, anticipating redeployment to the Pacific. The Army devised a point system to decide who could return home first. Points were assigned to a man's time in the service, participation in campaigns, medals received, whether or not he was wounded, and his marital status. This process was quite fair to the individual, but could be rather disruptive to the unit. The most experienced men were pulled from their companies, requiring their old units to fill the gaps with ill-trained replacements.[1]

Having the requisite number of points was no guarantee of an immediate trip home. "I knew people that had more points and still were in Europe."[2] Another year would pass before Corty could return to Schenectady. In August 1945 Cortland was sent to Paris to attend a two-week "boxing course." This wasn't training for the sport. He was learning how to package supplies for the Pacific campaign. "They sent us to school in Paris to pack our equipment. 'Pig Alley,' we called it. All

your GIs stayed there. And they told us to wear our clothes to bed or somebody would steal them, because the place was wide open."[3] This was *le Quartier Pigalle*, home to Paris's notorious nightspots.

Club Chipper, the Transportation Corps bar in downtown Antwerp. Left to right: Lee Harringer, Dave Weaver, Don Woods, Bernie Beals, Bruce Kramlich, and Bob Lipke in front. (DHW)

Between training sessions Cortland toured the city. "They had a restaurant in Paris named the Rainbow Corner."[3] He was a regular at this Red Cross club. It had opened shortly after the liberation of Paris and was a highly popular destination for American GIs. It was here on August 15, 1945 that Corty was relieved to hear Japan had surrendered to the United States. "I was in Rainbow Corners [sic] having lunch when they dropped the A-Bomb. So, they called us back to our units."[4] Some 519th men had already been redeployed to the Pacific, but there would be no need for Cortland to join that brutal fight.

TROUBLE WITH THE LOCALS

Their job done, thousands of American combat troops were returning from Germany. In June the Army constructed a camp to house up to 16,000 GIs while they waited to be shipped back to the States. Camp Top Hat was situated in a bend of the Sheldt River on the opposite side from the city. There were orders to stay in camp, but that didn't prevent bored soldiers from heading into Antwerp at night, carousing, drinking, and fighting. The exhilaration found in combat was replaced by excitement in town.[5]

One evening some 304th Port Company guys went to a local bar. While Corty sat down with a beer, his friend followed a girl to the far end of the bar. A couple of minutes later the GI ran out the door, chased by the Belgian girl's angry boyfriend. Cortland's fast-talking, fast-running friend wasn't hurt, but an incident like this shows why the troops were encouraged to drink at the military's servicemen-only clubs. As the volume of military materials flowing into Antwerp slowed, the port companies became idle and impatient. To keep morale high and the city peaceful the Army arranged dances, ball games, sightseeing tours, and extended furloughs. The recreational activities in Antwerp that began with the end of the V-weapon attack expanded greatly at the war's end.

SPORTS

A large number of 519th members were Wisconsin natives. These "badgers" formed a sports club. Their July 5, 1945 boxing show was reported back home four months later in the December 19, 1945 Green Sheet of the *Milwaukee Journal*:

> If you want to be a Badger, just come along with us to Antwerp, Belgium, where Wisconsin Servicemen sweating it out for home organized a Wisconsin Club of Belgium.... The group picture was taken at Rubens Palace in Antwerp, where the club entertained 7,000 servicemen at an outdoor sports show. Entertainers included Tenor Frank Eastwood ... and Luisette Daye, a Belgian dancer. For the first show the men built a ring out of oil drums and tank packing cases.[6]

The spring of 1946 saw the creation of a military softball league in Europe. Each of the companies were represented in the 519th Port Battalion team. The 519th's Historical Data Report was proud to report that their players did well:

> ...from the various companies a Battalion softball team was organized and when the preliminary rounds of the Com Z softball tournament started the 519th was entered. The 519th successfully

The 519th softball team, champions of Belgium, European Finalists. Top row: A. Notheis, P. Dottolo, R. Mendini, V. Warnes, B. Beal, R. Otto, P. McCarthy, E. Yahle, L. Markgraf, R. Kramer, Lt. G. Spronz. Bottom row: J. Bova, J. Shaughnessy, M. Kaplan, D. Bolton, J. Leone (manager), J. Simms, R. Raucci. (TJ)

The Wisconsin Club, composed primarily of 519th members. Matt Marvin (top row, far left), John Shireman (top row, middle), Dave Weaver (top row, center, in glasses), Bruce Kramlich (middle row in front of Weaver). (BCK) See www.519thPortBn.com for a full list of names.

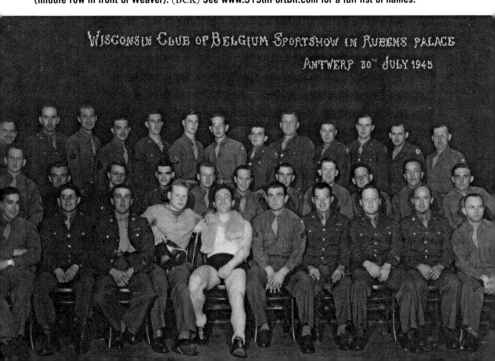

defeated all local contenders to the crown and emerged Port Area No. 3 champions. Through another series of games they became the Chanor Base representative for the Com Z tournament at Marseille. The entire team flew from Brussels to Marseille in a C-47 where they met teams from the various Base Sections, representative of hundreds of teams on the Continent. The 519th team, after winning its first two games in this tournament, ended the campaign finishing runner-up. This hard-working aggregation reflected fine spirit and credit upon the Battalion as a whole.[7]

FURLOUGHS AND PASSES

The 519th men were given passes to visit nearby sites. Cortland and Bruce Kramlich were both part of a group touring Napoleon's famous battlefield at Waterloo, Belgium. In Cortland's photographs one can see the GIs horsing around with Napoleonic and World War I objects at la Haye Sainte. One can be sure this sort of behavior is not tolerated by the modern-day museum curator. Enlisted men and officers were offered extended tours of Europe. Trips were planned to Copenhagen, Brussels, Paris, Holland, Switzerland, and the Riviera. Cortland was pleased to return to England. "They were actually giving away trips. I could have gone to Monte Carlo or Switzerland."[8] Yet, he took about a week to visit Marjorie's aunt and uncle in Norbury, a suburb of London. In the first week of December, Bruce Kramlich visited Switzerland, while Dave Weaver enjoyed the sunny Mediterranean in Nice, France.

A soldier from the Third Armored Division, Dave Weaver, and Delbert Staggs in Nice. (DHW)

Cortland, William Kelly, and other 519th men playing with museum objects at la Haye Sainte, Waterloo. (AJB)

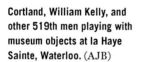

Ray Sonoski in Holland. He was joined by Dave Weaver, Bruce Kramlich, and Robert Lipke. (BCK)

THE BAND

After the skies were free of V-1s and V-2s it was safe for the battalion to institute regular parades. In March 1945 the troops marched every Friday afternoon to the music of the 519th band:

> Battalion weekly parades were inaugurated with music by the excellent military band of this organization. The military band was called on frequently for various reviews and presentations, and from the hard work that each individual member and the director put in to form this band came one of the best military bands in the Port Area, to ably represent the 519th Port Bn. The Battalion dance band was engaged in various Service Clubs and separate organizations sponsoring unit dances. This group also gave a day of their services each week to the 30th General Hospital, as did the military band when called upon.[9]

Five members of the military band formed a dance band called the "T S Capaders." In January 1945 they played for five enlisted men's dances and two officers' dances. Apparently quite popular, by March they were playing dances nightly and were visiting the hospital once a week. They entertained in each ward that held patients who could not leave their beds. Both the full military band and the dance band played musical shows for the American Red Cross.[10]

The 519th band playing at Camp McKay, Massachusetts. (BCK)

THE END OF THE 519TH

The 519th Port Battalion left Tampico Flats and relocated to the Luchtbal Barracks December 20, 1945. Its mission shifted completely to guard duty. The battalion began to disintegrate with the coming of the new year. Hundreds of men reached their requisite eighty-five points, earning them tickets home. On January 9, 1946 Bruce Kramlich, Dave Weaver, and many other 304th Port Company men left their duties in the port and were relocated to Camp Top Hat. Cortland Hopkins was redeployed to Le Havre, France around the same time. It seems that the 304th Port Company was disbanded and deactivated in this month. The spring of 1946 was very disruptive to the battalion. By March the last of the 305th Port Company's original members were lost through redeployment. Fresh replacements from the States and redeployed infantrymen filled in for the discharged men. Still, by April the company was trying to work at 50% strength. The 519th's other port companies were experiencing similar workforce losses. At the end of June, the 280th and 305th port companies were deactivated, with the remaining enlisted men transferred to two newly created companies, the 155th and the 285th. The 265th and 285th port companies were formed, and members of the 517th Port Battalion were absorbed into the 519th. The need for military guards diminished. On October 3, 1946 the entire outfit was deactivated.[11] The 519th Port Battalion that stormed Utah Beach and braved Antwerp's V-bombs was no more.

"Doughnut girls" serving the GIs at Camp Top Hat. (BCK)

15

HOMECOMING

As with Antwerp, the port at Le Havre, France had been an entry point for Allied supplies and reinforcements. With the end of hostilities in Europe, it became a center for the exit of military personnel. At the same time supplies continued to enter the port. American port units there were hampered by the loss of personnel. Experienced port company men were needed. In December 1945 or early January 1946 Cortland, Irving Sugarman, Ray Sonoski, and other 304th men were relocated to Le Havre. Sending these troops to disembark from France may have been intended to relieve the congestion in Antwerp. Cortland was quietly sitting in the packed train car when "This big guy came in. His arms were as big as telephone poles! He says, 'Hey soldier! Do you mind if I put you on the luggage rack, and I take your seat?' And, of course, I wasn't going to argue with him."[1] Cortland spent the last few hours perched up there with the barracks bags.

Upon his arrival in Le Havre, Cortland was assigned to manage the French civilian stevedores working the ship. "I didn't know anything about stevedoring, but according to the Army they had to have somebody there."[2] Although he served in a port company, Corty had no personal experience with that particular responsibility. In Antwerp he had only performed guard duty, and in Normandy he rarely worked off the DUKWs. He found working as a foreman in Le Havre an easy task. The job involved keeping an eye on the work, and that was about it.

As always, the availability of good food was greatly appreciated. While onboard he often struck up conversation with the sailors who "invited me in to have some coffee and sandwiches. It was better than what we were eating!"[3] This praise was echoed by Dave Weaver. "The one good thing about working on merchant ships was that we'd get into their mess hall, and maybe we'd get some food, and we'd always get coffee at least, and that was a big deal. Sometimes we'd have something even better than that. If you lucked out you might get a shower even!"[4] The French longshoremen were not all as friendly as the ship crew. Civilian casualties during the war and prolonged American military occupation placed a strain on the liberated countries, leading to a certain amount of resentment. It surprised Cortland when he got into an argument with his French crew, and "one of the stevedores said to me they were better off under the Germans!"[5]

Cortland had one last brush with danger before leaving Europe. One evening after work he was walking through the wharf back to his barracks. Entering the classic dark alley scenario, Corty was threatened by a group of local toughs. Cornered, Cortland lifted his jacket to reveal a handgun stuffed in his trousers. The men backed off. There had been reports in Le Havre of US personnel attacked by French men. Rumor held that an American had assaulted a French woman. The beatings were apparently a form of reprisal. Fortunately for Cortland, his sergeants had lent him a Luger for protection at night. American soldiers were not allowed to carry their weapons now that the fighting was over, but many men kept German pistols as souvenirs. A little shaken, Cortland got back to camp and was told the commanding officer wanted to see him. Corty thought, "What the hell did I do?" He wasn't in trouble. "He said to me 'I was going over your records and I was impressed. I have a good job for you. I want you to be a messenger for the duration of your stay here.' That was a good job."[6]

In the last weeks waiting to be shipped home Cortland worked as a courier. The guy who held the courier job before Corty told him it was *the best*. Cortland's duties were comparatively light and actually somewhat rare. He drove a jeep, chauffeuring officers and delivering packages. On one of his slow days he awoke from a nap and returned to his vehicle to find the spare tire had been stolen. This was a problem, because the cost of the lost tire would come out of his paycheck. Determined not to pay the fine, he headed over to the supply area. German prisoners worked there. He marched up to a man and told him to hand over a tire. The German requested official papers for the order. Corty pointed to his stripes and said, "*Here* are your orders!" Cortland got his tire. "An American would have told me to 'Go to Hell,' but those Germans knew how to take orders."[7]

The scattered 519th Port Battalion veterans returned home at different times. Larry Botzon was sent home on December 12, 1945. John Shireman had been allowed early discharge that month to see his ailing father. Bruce Kramlich and Dave Weaver sailed home from Camp Top Hat on January 12, 1946.[8] There is no record of exactly when Cortland finally left Europe. However, his arrival in Fort Dix, New Jersey, is documented as January 18, 1946. The 1944 sea voyage from New York to Liverpool had taken eleven days, so he probably boarded a ship in Le Havre on or around January 7th. "We were on board the ship about two days when the seas got very rough. I thought we were goners."[9] That storm would be the last of his adventures. His ship arrived in New York City, and he was transported to Camp Kilmer where he was discharged from service.

Boarding a ship for home at Camp Top Hat. (BCK)

Newlyweds Cortland and Marjorie. Her sister Olive appears at right. (AJB)

On January 23rd Cortland was riding a train to Schenectady. Completely unannounced, he walked through the front door to be greeted by his surprised and elated parents. Elder brother James had returned before him. Cortland called Marge on the phone, the two met the next day, and were married only weeks later. Younger brother Francis attended the wedding on furlough and was discharged not long after. All three Hopkins brothers were safely back home.

Returning servicemen across the country were eager to restart their lives. Cortland expected to get his old welding job, but he found Alco's workers on strike. This was just fine with the newlyweds. They took this as an opportunity for a long honeymoon. "We were married and drove to Jacksonville. We were gone about two weeks. When we got home the strike was over. I went to get my job, but they told me 'We don't have a job for you.'"[10] Cortland wouldn't stand for that. "When I went into the service they guaranteed my job." Cortland walked down to a nearby Veterans Affairs office and explained the situation. The US government wanted to shield its returning soldiers from economic hardship. Alco wasn't looking for workers, but the VA put on the pressure. Cortland was quickly rehired.

While some veterans were rewarded with government loans for college, Marge and Corty benefited from his service in the purchase of a new home. The GI Bill granted a zero downpayment and low-interest loan, allowing the excited couple to move out of Schenectady and into a house in suburban Rotterdam, New York. This happy little home was where they shared the rest of their lives. Here they would take in Marge's parents, raise two daughters, and entertain six grandchildren. Ever the volunteer, Cortland would continue to be active in his church and community. As time went by he would speak little of the conflict that so shaped his young life. Nearly seventy years after the war, Cortland Hopkins and the 519th Port Battalion veterans proudly discussed their history, and this author was honored to record it.

Cortland attending the dedication of the National World War II Memorial on May 29, 2004. (AJB)

EPILOGUE

One weekend some years after the war, Cortland's brother invited him to a bar. James wanted him to meet the owner, who had been a soldier at Utah Beach. Apart from the occasional letter or yearly Christmas card Cortland didn't really keep in touch with any of his old Army buddies, so meeting a fellow Normandy veteran intrigued him. The two sat down at the bar, the bartender was introduced, and Corty immediately noticed his accent. He was German. During the war the barkeep had been drafted into the German army, deployed to defend Utah Beach, and captured by the Americans. Now a US citizen, he was overjoyed to meet Cortland. "I drank for free all afternoon." There were no hard feelings at all. "He was doing his duty, and I was doing mine."

In contrast to Cortland, Bruce Kramlich's friends made an organized effort to stay in touch. Made up mostly of Midwesterners from the 304th Port Company, these veterans and their wives held numerous reunions. "We had several in Illinois, two in Michigan, several in Wisconsin, and two in Colorado. The last one was in 1995. There were fifteen or sixteen of us at the first reunions, but the number has gone down as we got older." The get-togethers included Robert Calfee, Tom Gardner, Harold Haack, LeeRoy Harringer, Richard Justice, Bruce Kramlich, Matt Marvin, John Shireman, Ray Sonoski, Dave Weaver, and Al Wiesbrock. Although there are no more organized reunions, the remaining old friends have made a point to continue to visit one another.

APPENDIX A: BATTALION HONORS

UNITED STATES DECORATIONS

European-African-Middle Eastern Campaign: This medal was awarded for service in the European theater of the war. The ribbon stripes were olive, green, white, red, and blue. Three small 3/16-inch bronze stars were pinned to the 519th Port Battalion men's ribbons. The stars represented participation in the campaigns in Normandy, Northern France, and the Rhineland. A small bronze arrowhead represented the 519th's participation in the amphibious assault at Normandy.

World War II Victory: All soldiers participating in the war received this medal. The ribbon featured a wide vertical red band with a rainbow of stripes on either side.

FOREIGN DECORATIONS

French Croix de Guerre 1939–1945: On May 25, 1945 the 1st Engineer Special Brigade and attached units received this honor for their participation in the Normandy Invasion. The ribbon was red with four vertical green stripes. A small bronze palm was pinned to the ribbon.

Decision No 758

The President of the Provisional Government of the French Republic, Commander of the Armies

Cites to the Command of the Army

"For exceptional services of war in the course of operations in Liberation of France"

The First Engineer Special Brigade, including all the units assigned to this Brigade or attached to it; who constituted part of Assault Force "U" and participated in the assault of the Normandy Beaches.

This citation includes the privileges of the Croix de Guerre avec Palme

Paris, 25 May 1945
(signed:) CHARLES DE GAULLE

General of the Armies, JUIN,
Chief of State - Major General
of the National defense.

The French Croix de Guerre was awarded to the 519th Port Battalion as a whole, allowing members of the 519th received ribbons to wear on their uniforms. The full medal with cross, however, was reserved for individual soldiers who were honored for specific actions. As a foreign decoration, the Croix de Guerre was typically omitted from US Army discharge papers.

Citation in the Order of the Day of the Belgian Army: The Belgian government officially expressed its gratitude to its American liberators in the Order of the Day of the Belgian Army. The document honored all the units and some noteworthy individuals who served in Belgium during the war. In 1948 an English translation was made available by a private publisher, Editions J. Rozez. Pages 80–81 of *Belgium Remembers and honors the U.S. Armies of Liberation, 1944-1945* by Colonel A. Baene lists the 13th Major Port and subordinate units stationed in Antwerp:

Decree of December 7, 1946, No 3254ter.

The Port Units of the armed forces of the United States in Service at the Port of Antwerp, who participated in the defense of the port and city against flying bombs, including:

Hq and Hq Detachment 519th Port Battalion;
Medical Detachment 519th Port Battalion;
302 Port Company;
303 Port Company;
304 Port Company;*
305 Port Company;
280 Port Company;
281 Port Company;
are mentioned in the Order of the Day of the Belgian Army, for:

The courage and devotedness which they showed by working without respite in the port of Antwerp during the terrible period of the V1 and V2 from October, 1944 to May, 1945, thereby saving the city and the port from almost complete destruction.

Military men or units receiving two mentions in the Order of the Day were eligible for the Belgian Croix de Guerre. The 519th Port Battalion, however, received only one mention.

---

*A typographical error in the book omitted the 304th Port Company from the list of honorees. Consulting an alternate translation confirms that the 304th was included in the original Order of the Day of the Belgian Army.

See www.519thportbn.com for the full list of port units based in Antwerp.

Certificate from the City of Antwerp: Perhaps the most treasured recognition received by the port battalion men was a personalized certificate awarded by the Antwerp city government. Cortland proudly framed his certificate, as did many of the men of the 519th.

THE PEOPLE OF
The City of Antwerp

To all to whom these presents shall come, greetings.
This certificate is awarded to

Corporal Cortland S. Hopkins 32941558

304th Port Company

in appreciation of, and as a token of gratitude for his work in the PORT OF ANTWERP during the one hundred seventy five days of continuous enemy air and V.-weapon attacks between October 7, 1944 and March 30, 1945.

Antwerp, 4th. September 1945.

ON BEHALF OF THE BOARD OF BURGOMASTER AND ALDERMEN:

By Order :
The Town Clerk,

The Burgomaster,

APPENDIX B: COMPANY ROSTERS

A 1973 fire at the National Archives St. Louis warehouse destroyed the bulk of World War II Army personnel records. Fortunately, Bruce Kramlich saved some documents from his time in headquarters. Among his papers was a list of Good Conduct Medal recipients. This list offers a near-complete list of men in each company as of August 1944. Officers did not receive the Good Conduct medal, so their names do not appear. Faded ink obscures some of the names on the document. Gaps in the roster have been partially filled by the memories of veterans and veteran families, a June 10, 1944 morning report, a December 1943 payroll record, and an August 15, 1945 notice of promotions. The 281st Port Company is completely absent, because it was attached after August 1945.

HEADQUARTERS

Officers

Maj. Charles H. Nabors
  (commander of the 519th)

Cpt. Glenn T. Foust, Jr.
  (medical detachment)

Cpt. Samuel Klauber (commander of
  the 519th Medical Detachment)

Cpt. Knauer

Cpt. F. W. Coykendall

Cpt. Andrew T. McGrath

Cpt. Nils A. Peterson

1st Lt. Joel Bornstein

1st Lt. Melvin Lutz

1st Lt. James L. Nobles

2nd Lt. William R. Henderson

Thurman F. Bowers (chaplain)

Enlisted Men

M/Sgt. Seymour Zeeman

T/Sgt. Edward C. Watson

1st Sgt. Alex Wanczak

Tec 3. Dallas K. Rudrud

Tec 4. Roger N. Lawrence

Tec 5. Edwin B. Byrom

Tec 5. Lawrence H. Botzon

Tec 5. Stanley M. Gadd

Tec 5. Matthew A. Marvin

Tec 5. Albert Wishner

Pfc. Richard B. Heist

Pfc. Bruce C. Kramlich

Pfc. Elwood C. McDonald

Pvt. Toivo H. Hamberg

Isaac Chancey

? Geyer

? Holngren

? Milliorn

Ralph Richard

279TH PORT COMPANY

S/Sgt
William H. Jackson, Jr.
Mordecai L. Solomon

Sgt
Henry J. Bachman
Michael C. Benicky
Reburn A. Epley
Henry J. Koch
Andrew D. Leggett
Emile A. Liberatore
William A. Mahoney
Greg Parente

Tec 4
Robert G. Dycus
Earnest W. Haynes
Claude H. Hinson
Albert J. Kremers
Charles R. Lusky
Raymond J. Mazzone
Andrew Muir
Peter J. Munley
Harold V. Putland
William E. Scanlon
Michael J. Walsh

Cpl
Anthony J. Barone
Harold Eisenberg
Winford H. Frick
Perry R. Hendrix
James A. Hindman
Harry Korslund
Benjamin Michniewicz

Tec 5
Albert J. Alogna
John F. Baer
Cosmo T. Barbaro
William R. Bennett
Solomon R. Bijou
Harry J. Blair
Tullio S. Brancaccio
Joseph W. Cervera
John J. Czinke
Clarence E. Evans
Alexander V. Feraro
Cager D. Finch
Rubin L. Gorewitz
Frank J. Gualtieri
Roy H. Hensley
Joseph M. Hunter
Howard M. Ingle
Sam Justice
John Koster
John Kowalski
Michael Krutz
Robert P. Lennox, Jr.
John E. Lucassen
Michael J. Maresca
Thomas C. McCrady
Frank R. McPike
Salvatore J. Moffa, Jr.
Joseph P. Neglia
Frank A. Nicholson
John J. O'Brien
Aloysius A. Pentony
George T. Ruggles
William J. Ryan, Jr.
Howard D. Stein

Murray Steinberg
Hugh J. Ward
William H. Welsh
Donald R. Wotton

Pfc
Rocco N. Alesandro
Robert J. Berg
Darwin A. Blake
Frank Bonanzo
Thomas J. Boyle
Saverio Bruzzi
Romuald Chodkowski
Samuel J. Cubito
Walter Davis, Jr.
Victor J. DeSantis
Bernard Donitz
John S. Eassy
William R. Eisenhauer
Frederick G. ?
Milton J. ?
Harold M. Haabestad
Dorsey H. Hard??
Joseph G. Harr?m
Tommie D. Harrison
James B. Hawkins
William Hecht
Leon C. Herd
Charles I. Hummer
Fred A. Icard
Herbert G. Israel
John W. Martin
Fred Meditz
John J. Millman
Angelo J. Minuti

Anthony M. Nicholais
Albert Olivetti
Benjamin C. Papapierto
Robert L. Ragan, Jr.
Pedro Rodon
Stanley Rethman
Gilfford E. Schmalia
Herbert Tepel
Joseph Trovato

Pvt

Charles A. Arnone
Frank L. Areassa
Michael J. Baiera
Joseph Barbitta
Joseph Belilos
William H. Binninger
Robert L. Bodarky
Edward J. Burns
Hector J. Consorte
James R. Dalton
Peter A. Del Greco
William Gibson
William T. Hagar
Robert W. Hankey
Virgile H. Harris
Julian C. Haselden

Cecil O. Hea?th
Paul M. Henderson
Claude H. Hendrickson
William H. Hunt
Walter N. Johnsen
Eli Kleiman
Jerome J. Manketo
Donald E. Mather, Jr.
Louis Nicotera
Mario A. Parisella
Arthur J. Savoy
Edward W. Szezecinski
Stanley S. Weir

280TH PORT COMPANY

1st Lt
William H. Collier

S/Sgt
Leo C. Bemis
Louis Esposito
Ernest L. Kluttz, Jr.
Harry S. Nix
James E. Taylor
William J. White

Sgt
James R. Arsenault
Edward S. Bettinger
Felix J. Chotkowski
Henry A. Ferrante
Edwin T. Ganung
William J. Millmore
Charles T. Padgett
Robert N. Palmer
Gerard A. Sullivan

Tec 4
Anthony J. Casalena
Arnold L. Gottlieb
Louis A. Grandjean
James G. Guariglia
Salvatore Ingoglia
Victor Kay
Warren F. Lollis
Raymond H. Maxie
Russell P. Moore
Mortimer J. Musnug
Howard Nelson
James F. O'Hara
Samuel I. Oster

Alvin H. Phillips
Enrico A. Starnadori

Cpl
Donald E. Cooper
Robert J. Corbett
Jacob Grubard
Harry O. Krumsick
(promoted to Sgt. in
August of 1945)
John H. McCoy
Steve M. McCracken
James E. Mosler
Samuel G. Paladino
(promoted to Sgt in
August of 1945)
Clarence D. Starr

Tec 5
Basil Auriemma
Fritz Bressel
Arnold A. Buehler
Emil G. Cappabianca
Alexander E. Carswell
Albert H. Christiansen
Fay E. Daley
Stanley J. Damulis
John DeStafanis
Raymond E. Fisher
John J. Fox, Jr.
Norman Gaiman
Anthony J. Galati
Nicholas Giardina
Thomas J. Ingrassia
Gustave H. Kahres
Louis R. Kinville
Charles B. Loving
(or Loying?)

George J. Machosko
Peter J. Martori
Denis J. McCarthy
Frank G. McCleod
Joseph Miano
David Mittlemann
Henry J. Mongarello
??? Kelse?
James Parris
Harry Permitin
Eurl Pierce
Herbert O. Pierson, Jr.
Howard E. Pike
Thomas E. Pryor
Edwin F. Radel
Charley G. Revis
Robert S. Roberts
Philip Schwartz
Merchant D. Slocum
Ben B. Stockard, Jr.
Edward J. Walters
Howard J. Whaley

Pfc
Robert E. Aydelotte
Irving Berkowitz
Sidney Buznitz
Stanley Caminiti
Louis P. Cici
Vincent J. Cordasco
Italo A. DeBartoli
Sam Dickson
Howard M. Donner
Stanley I. Dorsky
John M. Dunatov
Vito N. Ernest

Leonard F. Errico

Harry M. Fallick

Nat Feirstein

George E. Fox

William B. Freel

Charles Gallo

Salvatore Genovese

Francis J. Gesslein

John K. Gibbons

Norman Kalikow (transferred to the 280th in August 1945 from 734th Engr Hvy Shop Co.)

Charles Lee

Thomas Logan

Eugene A. Longhi

George S. Maggio

Carmin(e?) Maglia

Frank Magro

Harold Martin

Philip Martin

Conrad Masey

Edward Mathis

Anthony A. May

Thomas McCormick

Joseph Moscarello

Antonio C. Nunes

Willie R. Oakes

Ted J. Player

Nick Politakis

Isidore Primis

Peter C. Raffaele

Robert T. Rappa

William G. ·Ritzel

Anton A. Simmons

Peter Sloboda

Robert E. Stockland

Glynn R. Ward

Pvt

Jules Beslowitz

Johnie T. Bowman

Wayne C. Bradbury

Benjamin B. Bucario

Robert W. Clemons

David Cohen

Tony Covello

Frank L. Delia

David Y. Dember

Salvatore J. Durante

John A. Eaton

Lewis E. Eckstein

Richard L. Edwards

Russell R. Everman

Mario Favara

Nicholas Ferrar

Albert Fine

Lloyd W. Fowler, Jr.

Charles Frankel

David M. Fromowitz

James J. Gallagher

Norman Kalikow

John J. Krushewsky

Edward C. Latimer

William E. Lazar, Jr.

Leland E. Leonard

Louis J. Lopez

John V. Miske

Jayroe A. Moore

Ra...? Moskowitz

Guy Neathery

James O'Donnell

Edwin B. Pisani

Marion E. Pittman

Jesse A. Pointer

William J. Pollard

John W. Rogers, Jr.

Morris Rubnitz

J. B. Smith

Romaine A. Smith

Dick VanderKlok

Travis L. Wells

Daniel Wincheter

302ND PORT COMPANY

1st Sgt
Louis J. Finor

S/Sgt
Emory J. Branning
Stephan Davis
Raymond D. Flaxman
Harry Hervey
John M. Vincent

Sgt
Louis Bolas
Paul S. Bova
Roa?d H. Buerger
Edward F. Connors
Carlos M. Dixon, Jr.
Paul Pierce
Pete J. Connolly
Douglas Wilson

Tec 4
Cla??? Edwards
Thomas Edwards
Carl Hintzen
Lawrence Johnson
David J. Kitchen
Benjamin Manaseri
Alois A. Miller
Edward O. Moriarty
Leo A. Morin
Elmer F. Murphy
Elmer A. Peters
Daniel H. Rhinehart
John Sackman
Donald W. Schmelter
Alvin J. Schultz

Thomas H. Simac
James F. Simms
Theodore Strini
Robert L. Stevens
Ervin E. Weber

Cpl
Richard P. Chambers
Herbert W. Clarke
Milton M. Fieger
Frank J. Kaszubowski
Emil H. Lindstadt
Anthony J. Notheis
Raymond W. Otto
William O. Schlobohm

Tec 5
George Ackerle
Bernard B. Beal
Robert A. Benike
Raymond O. Bicknese
John R. Bowman
Harold K. Davids
August F. Eichorn
Paul Ftak
Frederick D. Gore
John M. Higgins
Claude A. Hutson
Ren L. Hutzel
Carroll G. Jamieson
Lyle A. Kobs
Robert H. Lerche
Henry Loesch
Clarence F. Marenda
Leroy W. Martin
Clemente M. Moraga

William T. Morrissey
Anthony Omerzu, Jr.
Henry A. Pawlak
Leonard H. Peschong
Virgil F. Radloff
Thomas Randazzo
Daniel Reeves
David Schaffner
John U. Schriner
Milton Schulman
Larry A. Schutlz
Leo H. Sherer
Edward T. Speakman
Robert E. Stone
Samuel A. Sorbo
Theodore C. Strini
Richard W. Tisdale
Raymond W. Troumbly
Clifford P. VanDoren
Emil A. Vigilio
Luke P. Walsh, Jr.
Robert F. Wiedenhoeft

Pfc
Edward Ackley
Robert D. Alby
Paul V. Anderson
James H. Aahton
William E. Augat
Omar E. Barry
Bernie G. Boring
Perfecto M. Cerventes
Albert E. Clifford
Noah L. Connolly
George A. Cool
Raymond C. Dasaro

Sam Dermer
Philip L. Erickson
Tom Foster
Dale K. Garlits
David A. Gleason
George J. Haller
John T. Havens
Joseph J. Hlivko
Merle E. Hughes
Anthony G. Kusinski
Arthur M. Lee
John R. McCormick
Thoms J. McPartland
Raymond W. Meador
Richard E. W. Olson
Ralph A. Riepl
Irving Rosenstreich
Lester Rosensweig
Courtney J. Sauter
Seymour Silver
Edward C. Skornog
Earl T. Taylor
James E. Tipp
John R. Turpin
George B. Wallis
Robert L. Ward
James E. Woods, Jr.

Pvt
George F. Barnes
Thaddeus S. Bialkowski
Clarence E. Gabrielson
John Gialto
Frederick B. Gilman
Arthur E. Grosser
Florian D. Kujawa
Braden E. Moore
Frederick L . Poetz
Casimer E. Prusinowski
Arnold R. Roecker
Robert L. Schreier
Joseph W. Schubert
Kenneth M. Swanson
Edward L. Troy
John Vanyo
Robert J. Wick
Frank Vena (or Vona?)
John Vandel
John Vanyo
Robert J. Wick

303RD PORT COMPANY

S/Sgt
first name? Bailey
C...? Dettloff
Raymond W. Villemure

Sgt
Edgar H. Bedard
Frank E. Eastwood
Irving Hoffman
Edmund T. Long
Frederick J. Wiegand

Tec 4
Roy Bridges
Virgil W. Bruce
Russel C. Burns
Donald L. Clark
Clarence W. Craver
George Dowhy
George Fox
Nicholas Fusco
Thomas J. Jur
Patrick J. McCarthy
Raymond D. Mendini
Robert W. Milliron
Charles F. Plank
Dick E. Viar
Robert L. Vonier

Tec 5
Gilbert A. Brossman
  (may have been in the
  304th at some point)
Howard R. Clark
Marvin O. Davis
Louis A. DeLuca
Charles R. DeRenzo

Raymond I. Dhesse
Harry R. Emanuel
Lincoln A. Frank
Maurice S. Giles
Isidore Goldberg
William H. Gramenz
Lawrence C. Hart
Ferd J. Hemmeter
Tony Horvat
Richard M. Icenhower
Martin J. Isaacson
Harry Israeloff
Russel F. Johnston
Walter Kaplan
Delos J. Kelley
Walter E. Lange
Clifford Lidskin
Paul E. Lytle
Edward McKiernan
Edmund G. Major
Norbert J. Moeller
Harold D. Moore
William L. Nusslein
Harold A. Peterson
Edwin M. Riedl
Clarence R. Strong
Robert J. Trainor
Edward J. Ulrich
Arthur A. Ware

Cpl
James T. Burke
George Plummer
John J. Shaughnessy
Edward R. Wandtke
Edward F. Yahle

Pfc
Walter J. Banaszak
Malcom F. Brenan
Edward T. Burns
Philip A. DeLuise
Peter A. Dottolo
Thomas W. Emerick
Walter F. Garlach
Albert DeLeonardis
Henry M. Gileta
Moe Gold
Edward J. Jasenovec
Arthur J. Jonuscis
Marshall O. Kenney
William Kumm
James C. Leone
Robert C. Letcher
Charles Lumer
Stanley J. Majeski
John J. McGee
Marvin B. Newman
Michael O'Kipney
Clifford H. Pickett
Robert M. Poeschl
Martin R. Pompa
John Rallis
Frederick J. Renner
Albert J. Ritta
Kenneth W. Roberts
Louis Rosenthal
Clyde E. Scott
Richard D. Skalecke
Frederick P. Tice
Vernon L. Warnes

Pvt

Rosario J. Abbinanti

Harry Chernicoff

Aubrey M. Differt

Elmer J. Ewig

Hyman Goldstein

John E. Hehnen

Charles S. Hirschman

Fred J. Iraggi

Benjamin Korn

Isadore H. Lentz

Angelo A. Lofaso

Maurice D. Luther

Joseph F. McCaskill, Jr.

William J. Pelton, Jr.

Felix C. Whitaker

David L. Wollner

304TH PORT COMPANY

1st Lt
William C. F. Lawler
(took command of
the company in
January 1945)

2nd Lt
John C. Winfree
? Gardner
? Renfrew

1st Sgt
Albert H. Bratzel

S/Sgt
James J. Dolan
(third platoon)
Willard J. LaBarge
Julian Schwartzberg
Delbert C. Staggs

Sgt
Samuel T. Scanlon
Donald W. Wood
Anthony Borkowski

Tec 4
John J. Cornacchi
Robert F. Lipke
Robert M. Marx
George? Massing
John O'Connor
(company clerk)
Palmer Perkins
Ralph F. Phelan
Ralph Ponomar?
Norman Radtke
Joseph Savarese

Edward Varnum
Efrain G. Vidaurri
David H. Weaver
William P. Wilder

Cpl
Donald L Hartung
George W. Klipfel
James J. Labita
Wilton M. Reavis
Edward L Smolen
Moubray Stoll
Clemens F. Uptmor, Jr.
Lawrence L. Wantland
John J. Wilson

Tec 5
Abelardo Alvarez
Morey Berger
Morris Bernstein
William H. Bowers, Jr.
Sylvester P. Dzikonski
Thomas A. Gardner, Jr.
Robert S. Gauron
LeeRoy C Harringer
Joseph B. Heinz
Cortland Hopkins
Edward J. Kaniewski
William J. Kelly
Steve J. Kocela
Richard C. Krause
Samuel Levine
Leslie Lilien
Joseph Maizlish
Earl E. Maloney
William V. McCullough

Thomas J. Reiter
Harry I. Ross
James F. Ryan
Joseph A. Schilling
William L. Schroeder
Arthur J. Schroedter
John E. Shireman
Raymond P. Sonoski
Charles Spencer
Roy O. S...?
Jack C. ???etzky
Thomas F. Viele
James L. Whitby
Aloysius C. Wiesbrock
Anthony V. Watson
Julius Zalesky

Pfc
Richard L. Baeten
Robert J. Ballenger
Philip Baratz
Edward Barlow
Edward G. Breitenfeldt
Alvin J. Brettman
Allen P. Boegner
George W. Cagle
Richard H. Chitty
Howard E. Clark
Wallace C. Gilbert
Harold J. Haack
Raymond D. Hankins
Lloyd H. Hoover
Richard J. Justice
Albert J. Karowski
Morris E. Klinger
Herbert P? Koller

Franklin W. Lentz
Anthony J. Litvin
Walter McKinney
Louis M. Oromaner
Dominic C. Parise
James O. Ruidl
Lyle M. Schlekau
Melvin E. Schon
John E. Stonestreet
Israel Sugarman
Edward ?. Vitkovich
Johnnie A. Williams
Robert R. Woodcock
Morris Yohai

Pvt
Francesco Barone
Nicholas A. Cannone
John Crupi
James E. Curry
Albert L. DiJohn
Hartley G. Husted
Andrew J. Kostur
Sidney H. Kraus
Vernsley G. McLaughlin
Harold B. Pollack
Frank Rodriguez
Kurt Schiff
Benjamin Sherman
Walter M. Slasinski

Leo Sommer
Lionel L. Ridgeway
Robert C. Sorenson
Jack J. Swope
Irwin Tobe
Dwayne E. Trantham
Peter J. Tyrcha

**Unknown rank
in August 1944**
Harley Baily
Robert G. Calfee
Roger Deane
Michael DeLaura
Verle W. Hamilton
James McConchie
Gilbert Mello (Mellow?)
Rick Pinicotti
Ken Roberts
Woodrow Wilson

305TH PORT COMPANY

1st Lt
Dominick P. Apone
James L. Nobles

S/Sgt
Charles Mercuric
William F. Sheehan

Sgt
Herbert E. Crampton, Jr.
William M. Foyle
Charles C. Maxwell, Jr.

Tec 4
Roy E. Carter
Robert M. Dawson
Lester S. Faine
James F. Golembowski
Sol Hoffman
Robert B. Holmgren
Edwin Lornson
Charles J. Mahoney
Kenneth D. McDaniel
James M. Oldani
Howard S. Pinkston
Joseph A. Rosenberger
Gerald T. Smith
David Spartz
Joseph J. Toscano
Frederick T. ???war?
James C. Trudeau
John Zaher

Cpl
Floyd H. Coles
Rayond Gagnon

Raymond Goodson
Henry Kaiser
Emil H. Krueger
Robert B. Nelson

Tec 5
Ervie Anderson
Trygve Benson
David Bolton, Jr.
Bernard J. Brown
Abraham M. Chudnow
Theodore E. Darrow
Albert J. DeSimone
Aaron Dorfman
Charles H. Eichenberg
Joseph R. Farina
Leonard J. Giordano
Herman W. Gorsky
Morris Greenberg
Leonard Henigson
Eliot L. Hirsch
Bertram L. Kime
Deane A. Knapp
Henry E. Lee
Farrell E. Lykins
Leroy J. Markgraf
Biagio A. Masturzo
Waldron G. Meyers
Wayne O. Neff
LaVerne Olsen
Arthur H. Opsahl
Edward D. Ryan
Frank A. Sacco
Herman A. Schneider
Abraham A. Siegel
Gordon A. Spitzer

Robert M. Stift
Albert M. Trapp
John C. Trione
Norman R. Will

Pfc
Wallace L. Blodgett
Timothy J. Cavey
Michael A. Coleman
William H. Draeger, Jr.
Harold G. Ehlers
Cleo I. Foster
Kurt Fuld
Joseph Grosso
Michael Haberern, Jr.
Lawrence E. Hull
George Immekus
Clifford R. Johnson
Melvin Kaplan
Murray Kimler
John P. Macukas
Raymond E. Mallard
Michael M. Mangini
Arthur J. McMullen
Erwin L. Miller
William G. Oberlander
Wallace J. Oden
William L. Page
Frank Pasore
Meyer Penn
Loyd B. Pitts
Raymond A. Rappa
James A. Read
Joseph A. Rogan
Stanley J. Roicki, Jr.
Eldor A. Rosenow

George J. Sciascia
Ernest Sokel
John T. Swaim
Steve A. Talaski
Martin F. Whetsell
Pvt
Raymond L. Boyd
Harold E. Britton
Duane I. Brockway
Chester E. Cordts
Thomas Desmond
Andrew J. Feliton, Jr.
Jacob Fox
Edgar A. Griefendorf
William P. Groth
Russell W. Hess
Walter J. Holston
Sam Lerner
Jack R. Leskey
James J. Lyons
Stanley Manilow
Max Margolis
Frank McKenna
Gerald E. McLin
Walter Mensinger
Jack Pierce
Rupert J. Pomper
Orlando Rodriguez, Fr.
Leon Rosenfeld
Norman Rosenzweig
Conrad F. Schneider
Arthur E. Tewes
Harris J. Winkelstein

APPENDIX C: 519th PORT BATTALION INSIGNIA

Amphibious Training Command
The 519th received this shoulder patch after it was attached to the 1st Engineer Special Brigade. The eagle, gun, and anchor are yellow on a blue background. It was worn on the right shoulder.

Engineer Amphibious Command
The 519th received this shoulder patch after it was attached to the 1st Engineer Special Brigade. The seahorse is red. The border is blue, and the background is white. On a jacket it was worn on the left breast.

European Theater of Operations, US Army (ETOUSA)

After the formation of the Supreme Allied Headquarters in February 1944, ETOUSA focused on the administration and supply of US troops. The insignia represents this function by incorporating the blue star and white petal-shaped field of the Service of Supply (SOS). The US Army's Transportation Corps was a part of the SOS.

US Army Transportation Corps
This emblem appeared on dress uniform lapel pins, unit flags, and various other objects.

APPENDIX D: 519th PORT BATTALION HISTORICAL DATA REPORT

The following is a history of the 519th Port Battalion written in 1946.
It is included among the unit's documents held at the National Archives.
Numerous officers signed the battalion's monthly historical reports, while the
author of this record was not indicated. Misspellings in the text have been
corrected, and some paragraph breaks have been inserted.

Headquarters
519th Port Battalion
APO 562, U.S. Army
Historical Data Report

Upon activation of the Battalion on 25 June 1943, assigned
officers and cadre were without personnel to commence a regular
basic military training program until arrival of the main body of
recruits from Reception Centers at Camp Grant, Illinois and Camp
Upton, New York on July 19 1943 and 3 August 1943 respectively.

Regular training schedules went into effect on 20 July 1943 and
recruits assigned to organization on subsequent dates were placed in
special groups under direct supervision of Training Center S-3. The
military training of the two groups was coordinated to the extent
that the Battalion as a whole completed the prescribed schedule of
military subjects on about 30 August 1943.

Upon completion of the course in military subjects the Battalion
began technical training in Port Battalion work as prescribed by
Training Program 55-1. In addition to classroom instruction, the
course included actual work and training on "landships" (cargo ships
and dock facilities complete with cargo and gear—built on land in the
camp area.)

Hatch and dock crews were trained in procedure as practiced by
civilian stevedores and longshoremen. This consisted of breakdown
of each platoon into three 21-man sections under the supervision of

a buck sergeant. These sections were composed of 1 section leader, 2 winch operators, 1 signalman, 1 cargo checker, 1 hatch foreman, 1 dock foreman, 2 slingers, and 12 longshoremen. Training included both loading and unloading procedures.

The training program consisted entirely of dock-side operations and did not include the amphibious type of operations of unloading cargo from ship to ferrying craft.

During this period of technical training additional specialized military subjects were completed by the entire Battalion.

1. Gas Chamber
2. Infiltration Course
3. Small Arms AA Fire
4. Carbine familiarization firing
5. Extended marches and bivouacs.

On 17 October the Battalion moved to Camp Myles Standish, Massachusetts where, during a 10-day stay, men with incompleted courses of training were brought up to par with the balance of the unit; a schedule of transition firing on the rifle range and familiarization firing of the grenade launcher begun for the Battalion.

On the 25th of October the organization moved via bus and truck to the Army base for further technical training prior to overseas assignment.

However, due to the unusual labor situation that existed in Boston, it was impossible to secure the necessary training. Each company was given a short training period aboard a ship which had been set aside by the Port Authorities for use by Port Battalions. In addition to this it was occasionally possible for sections to load live cargo when the civilian longshoremen discontinued work because of rain or cold weather.

By using the sections as labor crews in unloading boxcars, handling supplies in the warehouses and acting as clean-up crews aboard the ships, the Battalion was able to supplement the permanent troops in the Port in clearing a record tonnage thru Boston during the winter months.

Morale was at its lowest ebb during this period. The soldiers who were working alongside of civilians that received five times their pay, frequently complained that they had been urged by these same civilians to "slow up" and "take it easy".

It is hard to note any advantage of a military nature that was derived from the five month stay in this area. For reasons mentioned above, technical training was negligible and facilities for military training were inadequate both from a plant and cooperation standpoint. However, it was possible at this time for company commanders to sort out the best of their non-coms and realign their company structure for the harder task that they knew was to follow.

After staging from 2 March 1944 to 23 March 1944 at Camp Myles Standish, the Battalion sailed for the ETO, arriving at Liverpool, England on 5th April 1944. thence moving to Bristol, Gloucestershire where it was assigned work at the Avonmouth docks under supervision of the 17th Major Port.

It was at this station that the Battalion first loaded live cargo in an appreciable quantity. Despite their very apparent lack of experience, the work crews received many commendations from Port authorities for their enthusiasm and spirit of cooperation.

Efforts were made while in Bristol to secure assignment to some of the Amphibious problems that were taking place at several points along the coast. These efforts were unsuccessful, and to insure that the Battalion should function properly in performing its mission on the beaches of Europe, key officers and NCO's were given instruction in some of the problems that were likely to arise in an amphibious operation.

Work conditions in Bristol were such that it was decided that 18-man work sections were more feasible than the 21-man sections employed in the U.S. This was possible, not only because of the use of the dock side cranes, but also because of increased efficiency on the part of the men once they gained experience.

Transportation and feeding of the work sections proved to be the most difficult administrative problems to be solved. The organizational transportation was at all times woefully inadequate and trucks had to be borrowed from other units to perform normal administrative functions.

By assigning to one enlisted man the sole job of arranging transportation, it was possible to have fairly efficient around-the-clock service.

The food handling problem was more difficult to solve and eventually permission was secured to obtain enough additional Marmite cans to serve hot food to all sections working on the docks.

For invasion purposes the primary mission of the Port Battalion was the discharge of cargo from ships onto ferrying craft for transfer to supply dumps on shore. To accomplish this mission the Battalion left the marshaling areas of the UK with various companies, platoons, and sections assigned to numerous Liberty ships, freighters, and coasters of the invasion fleet. Each section was assigned the job of discharging their respective vessels upon arrival at the "far shore". Cargo included personnel, combat loaded vehicles, ammunition, petrol, Air Force, Engineer, QM, Ordnance, and Medical supplies.

Upon completing discharge of their respective vessels, units came ashore and assembled in a bivouac area five hundred yards back from high water. From Headquarters CP in this area section work assignments to other ships was continued.

Unloading operations proceeded twenty-four hours a day, and aboard ship, in transit, and in the beach head bivouac area, the Battalion was subjected to enemy aircraft bombing and long range artillery fire. The only complete cessation of operations was caused, not by enemy action, but by the four day storm which swept the beach head making landing operations impossible for all craft other than the large LST's which were able to beach at high tide and discharge cargo and personnel directly on land during low tide periods.

The only Battalion battle casualties were suffered during the first week of landing operations on the continent. All the victims of aerial bombing. Of the total number of casualties (22), there were 10 killed and 12 wounded. Casualties occurred both aboard ship where sections were working and in the bivouac area.

On 24 June the Battalion moved to a new bivouac area to the north and inland from the place of the original landings. To facilitate unloading operations thru closer contact with the Navy Beach Battalion CP, and the Army Beach Operations Section, a Battalion Operations CP was established in a cached enemy pillbox on the beach. From this CP came all work orders and reports having to do with Battalion activity on the water. The original mission of this Battalion Beach CP was to set up and operate a control station to coordinate and facilitate the demands of the 1st Engineer Special Brigade and the Navy and in this it was successful. This type of operation had not been tried before and its success and subsequent adoption by other similar units was proof of need of this sort of an operation where a Battalion was given complete responsibility for a specified section of the beach.

Coming ashore in France the Battalion was without any T/E equipment, gear or vehicles. Contrary to the planned methods of operations, some ships reaching the beachhead did not have adequate or proper gear aboard to properly and efficiently discharge their respective cargos. This necessitated improvisation and extra work on the part of officers, section leaders, riggers, and men working as longshoremen. The acute shortage of ready gear at this critical time was only solved by the establishment of a Battalion gear shop. The shop was set up with experienced riggers in charge, and with whatever material was available. The main work was splicing cable and turning out chokers, ranging in sizes capable of carrying light cargo or the medium tanks. After the initial call for gear had been met and there was time to try other projects, heating systems for mess facilities, shower baths, and vehicle maintenance were planned and completed as part of the regular work.

A new type of hook for unloading landing mats, patterned after the type used at the air corps dumps was made by the Battalion riggers. Each set of hooks were made from two sections of junked heavy tank treads. These landing mat hooks as developed for use with ships gear speeded unloading operations 40% on this one type of vital cargo.

Several methods for unloading 155 MM ammunition were tried by the sections. It was found possible to substantially increase the loads that could be removed with each lift by using double rope slings, as compared with the accepted practice of using hooks on each shell.

During one period of operations when discharge of supplies badly needed on shore from a Liberty Ship was being held up due to lack of barges to remove accumulated dunnage, hatch crews built a raft with the dungaree, lowered it over the side, loaded it with remaining dunnage and proceeded with other unloading as soon as a tug came alongside and towed the raft toward shore. This raft method of getting cargo to shore was used successfully when sealed tanks handicapped and slowed unloading because of their size.

After the Battalion had moved back away from the beach to its new bivouac area, the problem of getting men from the area to the beach was an ever increasing one. If transportation from the DUKW co's stationed nearby, or the truck Co's in the area was not available, it meant the men had to leave the area an hour earlier than their scheduled shift time, and walk to the beach in order to arrive at the DUKW Co's dispatch offices in time to work their required shift. An hours walk, 12 hours of work and then the hike back to the area, continuing day after day made the change in T-E with the allotment of vehicles to each Co most welcome. The new T-E gave to each Co additional vehicles, and all were consolidated and operated under a Battalion Motor pool for the mutual advantage of all phases of Bn. operation. In spite of the fact that the DUKW co's were stationed nearby, and did have a number of DUKWs continually running from the dispatch officers-on the beach to within a few hundred yards of the Bn. bivouac area, it was with difficulty that any cooperation whatsoever was obtained in transporting men to and from work. It was at this same time that the T-O was changed for Port Co's, cutting the men in a section from 21 to 16. If discharge work did not require a crew of men on the craft being loaded, it was found that by cutting the sections still further, to a figure below the 15 man section was possible, allowing more hatches to be worked. Tonnage figures were appreciably increased by this move, not working any additional hardships on the men.

During the last two months on Utah Beach the weather caused numerous stoppages in the amphibious unloading operations. These stoppages varied in duration from one to five days. During the first two weeks in November it was possible to work the beach only seven days. During rough weather crews were kept on an alert status in the bivouac area ready to board ships at the first break in the weather. Storms often struck with no warning and sections were stranded on board ship for the duration of the storm. For this reason all crews carried emergency rations when going aboard. The sections crews of this battalion ceased operations on Utah Beach on 12 November 1944. The figures and statistics given here were compiled from Battalion tonnage reports forwarded twice daily to Beach Operations.

The Battalion received verbal orders to move from Utah Beach via train to Antwerp on the 13th of November and entrained at Chef-du-Pont, France 24 hours later. The train journey was uneventful and the unit arrived in Antwerp on the evening of 18 November 1944. The first four days at this station were utilized in cleaning up the barracks, the area, and the men's equipment. The battalion received material aid in this through the excellent cooperation of both the 487th Port Battalion and the Headquarters of the Port Troops Commander at Luchtbal Barracks. On 22 November the Battalion began furnishing men in the quantity for various fatigue and guard details upon order from Port Troops. As is usual at the inception of an operation of this type, many difficulties were encountered in coordinating the actual number of men needed on these details with the number called for, in arranging transportation and food, and various other administrative problems. the first ships arrived in Port of Antwerp on 30 November 1944 and the Battalion sent the first of its work crews to the docks to supervise civilian stevedores in the discharge of cargo. At the end of November the Battalion was furnishing 177 men as security dock guards daily and 360 men daily for work on the docks, with 168 men engaged to various details throughout the Port as drivers, clerks, and mobile equipment operators.

The greater part of December 1945 was spent in adjusting and reorganizing its personnel to the job of obtaining maximum tonnage with the facilities at hand. Apparently no specific plan for the utilization of military stevedores existed until the first ships actually arrived in Antwerp and lack of such plan meant that many field expedients in the matter of supervision and control had to be used. The expedient that was used successfully was the assumption of responsibility in certain dock areas by individual companies with the company commanders assuming the responsibilities ordinarily those of officers in charge of the docks. It was observed that the allotting of specific areas to specific companies had increased the efficiency of that company. Men and officers took personal and increased interest in the work as a matter of organizational pride. By the end of December 1944, the Battalion was furnishing an average of 248 dock guards daily and men for dock personnel numbered 500 per day. In addition to these two main operations, men were furnished as drivers and dispatchers for the 13th Port, train guards, a daily detail of 12 men for the APO, PX clerks, clerks in the Adjutant's and Provost Marshall's offices at Luchtbal Barracks.

The V weapon attack on Antwerp had increased since the Battalion arrived in Antwerp, but the efficiency and alertness of the members of this Battalion was increased steadily in an effort to move all cargo. Personnel were assigned positions of much greater responsibility, as civilian employees conducted operations under supervision of military authority. The relations of employees and military personnel were satisfactory, and the coolness and devotion to duty evidenced by military personnel under the adverse conditions produced a steadying influence on the civilian workers to the end that stoppages or slow downs in operation due to enemy activity was held at a minimum. The labor breakdown for the month showed 215 dock guards daily plus 45 train guards sent out, an average of 150 checkers a day, the regular port details which were permanent and supervision other than checkers amounting to about 350 a day.

Work by the four companies on the docks and the two companies pulling security guard continued with few interruptions during the month of February. Some labor difficulty was encountered by strikes of civilian workers, but increased effort on the part of military labor kept lost time at a minimum. The V Weapon attack continued and reached its highest point of effectiveness during this month. The Battalion was fortunate in not sustaining any serious casualties, but minor injuries brought on by cuts received by flying glass were numerous. The Battalion furnished all men available during the month and aided materially in making this the biggest month for cargo discharge in the Port of Antwerp.

Three companies continued to work dock areas during the month of March, two companies continued to have security guard, and one company was assigned to duties of guarding the Kruisschans Sluis area. This guard necessitated the establishment of separate billets, and mess facilities as it was impossible to continue the guard efficiently from the Company Area at Tampico Flats. The guard included manning of 50 cal. machine guns and placing depth charges in strategic positions in accordance with instructions. Personnel on the docks coordinated all work, including ordering and loading rolling stock and barges, ordered and directed civilian labor in all ship discharge, and did it in such a manner as to contribute greatly to the record discharge up to that time.

Battalion weekly parades were inaugurated with music by the excellent military band of this organization. The military band was called on frequently for various reviews and presentations, and from the hard work that each individual member and the director put in to form this band came one of the best military bands in the Port Area, to ably represent the 519th Port Bn. The Battalion dance band was engaged in various Service Clubs and separate organizations sponsoring unit dances. This group also gave a day of their services each week to the 30th General Hospital, as did the military band when called upon.

Regular work for the Battalion continued and with the end of the V Weapon attack on Antwerp, recreational facilities in the

Port Area were increased. The Battalion fulfilled quotas called for in transferring men to Reinforcement Depots for re-training as combat troop reinforcements. The replacements came in and were given parallel on-the-job training with the established key men that remained and were actively engaged in discharge work on the docks. Seven highly qualified enlisted men of the Battalion were granted direct commissions as second lieutenants and there were numerous applicants for Infantry OCS.

The furlough and pass schedule was increased by quota allotted by Chanor Base Section and Officers and EM were given the opportunity to visit England, Paris, Brussels, Riviera, and Switzerland. Post activities were increased to include a post theater, canteen, library, and a recreation hall.

An athletic program to include all units of the post was organized and each company was represented in the softball league. Bad weather, constant changing of personnel, and the unavailability of players at scheduled games because of dock work prevented the completion of the schedule. However, from the various companies a Battalion softball team was organized and when the preliminary rounds of the Com Z softball tournament started the 519th was entered. The 519th successfully defeated all local contenders to the crown and emerged Port Area No. 3 champions. Through another series of games they became the Chanor Base representative for the Com Z tournament at Marseille. The entire team flew from Brussels to Marseille in a C-47 where they met teams from the various Base Sections, representative of hundreds of teams on the Continent. The 519th team, after winning its first two games in this tournament, ended the campaign finishing runner-up. This hard-working aggregation reflected fine spirit and credit upon the Battalion as a whole.

APPENDIX E: TIMELINE

1943

June 25
519th Port Battalion activated at
Indiantown Gap, Pennsylvania.
Major William G. Lefferts assumed
command.

August 2
Major Charles M. Nabors
assumed command.

October 17
Left Indiantown Gap.

October 18
Arrived at Camp Myles Standish,
Massachusetts.

October 25
Left Camp Myles Standish.
Arrived at Boston Army Base.

November 14
Moved to Camp McKay in
South Boston.

1944

March 2
Left Camp McKay. Arrived
at Camp Myles Standish.

March 23
Left Camp Myles Standish, arrived
at Commonwealth Pier, and
boarded the SS *Edmund B.
Alexander*.

March 24
Sailed from Boston.

April 4
Arrived at Port of Liverpool,
England.

April 10
Left Liverpool.

April 11
Arrived in Bristol, England.

April 13
Commenced work at
Avonmouth Docks.

May 4
280th Port Company attached.

May 13
279th Port Company attached.

May 31
Left Bristol and arrived at
marshalling area at
Bridgend, Wales.

June 2
Left marshalling area and arrived
at Newport, Wales. Boarded ships
of the invasion fleet. The 303rd
Port Company was split and
boarded ships at Avonmouth and
Southampton, England.

1944

June 6
Fleet arrived off the coast of Normandy, France.

June 7, 8, 9, and 10
Battalion arrived on Utah Beach.

October 7
German V-weapon bombardment of Antwerp, Belgium began.

November 12
279th Port Company released.

November 14
Battalion departed from Ravenoville, France via truck and DUKW to Chef-du-Pont.

November 15
281st Port Company attached.

November 18
Arrived at Antwerp and assigned to the 13th Major Port. Billeted in Tampico Flats.

1945

March 30
Last V-weapon landed in Antwerp.

May 7
Germany surrendered.

August 15
Japan surrendered.

December 20
Battalion relocated to the Luchtbal Barracks.

1946

October 3
519th Port Battalion deactivated.

APPENDIX F: PORT BATTALION ORGANIZATION

The US War Department's 1943 *Stevedoring and Wharf Handling* manual presented three charts outlining the composition of a port battalion headquarters, port battalion, and port company. In actual practice there could be departures from the ideal. For instance, the 519th Port Battalion was commanded by a major, rather than a lieutenant colonel. The 519th included six port companies, rather than the suggested four.

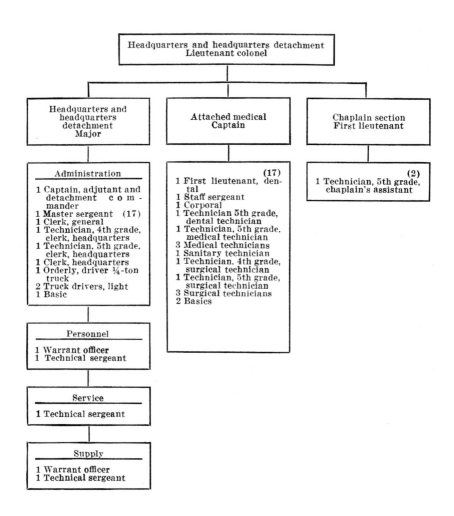

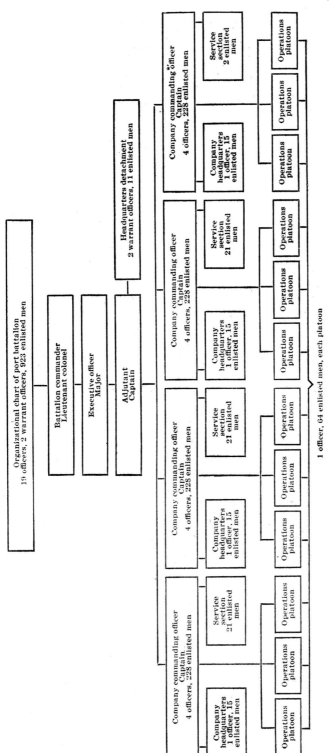

Organizational chart of port battalion
19 officers, 2 warrant officers, 923 enlisted men

Battalion commander
Lieutenant colonel

Executive officer
Major

Adjutant
Captain

Headquarters detachment
2 warrant officers, 11 enlisted men

Company commanding officer
Captain
4 officers, 228 enlisted men

Company
headquarters
1 officer, 15
enlisted men

Service
section
21 enlisted
men

Operations
platoon

1 officer, 64 enlisted men, each platoon

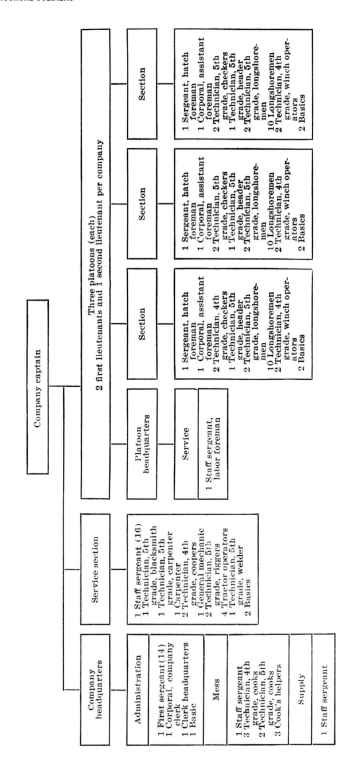

NOTES

CHAPTER 1: SCHENECTADY

1. Hopkins, interview by author.
2. These inexpensive shops were the precursor to the modern dollar store. Kresge's company would eventually become K-Mart department store.
3. Hopkins, interview by author.
4. Francis' ship was the USS LCS(L)(3)-112. For more information see Robin L. Rielly. *Mighty Midgets at War: The Saga of the LCS(L) Ships from Iwo Jima to Vietnam* (Central Point, OR: Hellgate Press, 2000) and Donald L. Ball. *Fighting Amphibs: The LCS(L) in World War II.* (Williamsburg, VA: Mill Neck Publications, 1997).
5. Hopkins, interview by author.
6. Ibid.

CHAPTER 2: AMERICAN LOCOMOTIVE COMPANY

1. Wilkin, "M-7 Remembered."
2. American Locomotive Company, *Growing With Schenectady....* .
3. *Schenectady Gazette*, "Ingenuity Used at Alco in Building First Tank"; *Schenectady Gazette*, "Alco Produced 1st Med. Tank 2 Years Ago."
4. *Schenectady Gazette*, "Howitzer Combined with Tank Chassis."
5. *Schenectady Gazette*, "Ingenuity Used at Alco in Building First Tank."
6. Bagnato, interview by author, June 19, 2007; Wilkin, "M-7 Remembered."
7. American Locomotive Company, *Growing with Schenectady.*
8. Hopkins, interview by author.
9. Nomination for Navy "E" Award by Bureau of Ordinance.
10. *Schenectady Gazette*, "Alco Here Wins 3 Awards for Production."
11. *Schenectady Gazette*, "These Honors to Go to Alco Plant, Employees."
12. Letter from Alco president, Duncan W. Fraser, to Rear Admiral H. A. Wiley, USN, May 27, 1942.
13. *Schenectady Gazette*, "These Honors to Go to Alco Plant, Employees."
14. *Schenectady Gazette*, "Alco and 8,000 Workers Receive 'E' Award Today."
15. Belkin, "Lucy Monroe Dies."
16. *Schenectady Gazette*, "Alco and 8,000 Workers Receive 'E' Award Today."
17. Ibid.
18. Ibid.
19. Ibid.

20. "It's M-7 Day," a full-page ad on p. 14 of the *Schenectady Gazette*, April 10, 1943.

21. *Schenectady Gazette*, "Schenectady Kept Secret of Tank Killer."

22. M-7 Day Program on front page of *Schenectady Gazette*, April 10, 1943.

23. Ibid.

24. *Schenectady Gazette*, "M-7 Praised by British Colonel."

25. Ibid.

26. Ibid.

27. Ibid.

28. Ibid.

29. *Schenectady Gazette*, "Churchill, F.D.R. Acclaim 'Desert Victory'"; *Schenectady Gazette*, "M-7 Praised by British Colonel." After the film there was a reception at the Hotel Van Curler for special guests.

CHAPTER 3: IN THE ARMY NOW

1. Hopkins, interview by author.

2. Ibid.

3. Ibid.

4. Ibid. It is interesting to note that during these years Cortland was under the false notion that his middle name was Frank. Consequently, all his military records would bear the name Cortland "F." Hopkins. Corty's parents did not have a copy of his birth certificate. It was only in the year 2000 that his daughter, Patti, tracked down a copy of his birth certificate, proving his middle name was Oliver.

5. Rothrock, *Indiantown Gap Military Reservation.*

6. Ibid.

7. Ibid.

8. Ibid.

9. Hopkins, interview by author.

10. Historical Data Report. Headquarters, 519th Port Battalion.

11. Hopkins, interview by author.

12. Kramlich, correspondence with author

13. Shireman, correspondence with author.

14. Sonoski, interview by author.

15. Weaver, correspondence with author.

16. Ibid.

17. Ibid.

18. Hopkins, interview by author.

19. Historical Data Report. Headquarters, 519th Port Battalion, 1946; *War Department Training Manual No. 55-310.*

20. Davis, "Training Transportation Corps."
21. *War Department Training Manual*, No. 55-310.

CHAPTER 4: BOSTON

1. Historical Data Report. Headquarters, 519th Port Battalion.
2. Ibid.
3. Hopkins, interview by author.
4. Colley, *The Road to Victory*.
5. Hopkins, interview by author.
6. Ibid.
7. Ibid. Charge of Quarters (CQ) was the duty to do with checking passes.
8. Shireman, interview by author.
9. Gawne, *Finding Your Father's War*.
10. Hopkins, interview by author.

CHAPTER 5: THE ATLANTIC

1. Historical Data Report. Headquarters, 519th Port Battalion.
2. Hopkins, interview by author.
3. Sugarman, interview by author.
4. Cortland, interview by author.
5. Shireman, correspondence with author.
6. Kramlich, correspondence with author.
7. Hopkins, Interview by author.
8. Ibid.

CHAPTER 6: ENGLAND

1. Historical Data Report. Headquarters, 519th Port Battalion.
2. Hopkins, interview by author.
3. Historical Data Report. Headquarters, 519th Port Battalion.
4. Weaver, interview by author.
5. Historical Data Report. Headquarters, 519th Port Battalion.
6. Morse, *A Moment in History*.
7. Sonoski, interview by author.
8. Hopkins, interview by author.
9. Penny, "The Luftwaffe over Bristol, 1941–1944."
10. Shireman, interview by author.
11. Penny, "The Luftwaffe over Bristol, 1941–1944."
12. Hopkins, interview by author.
13. Colley, *The Road to Victory*.

14. Higgs, "Delphine's War."
15. Shireman, interview by author.
16. Historical Data Report. Headquarters, 519th Port Battalion.
17. Weaver, interview by author.
18. Morrison, "Port Men Truly Sweat Out Invasion"
19. Shireman, interview by author.
20. Sugarman, interview by author.
21. Bykofsky and Larson, *United States in World War II*, pp. 110-111.
22. Hopkins, interview by author. In England at this time a cellar temperature of 50-55°F was preferred.
23. Ibid.
24. Army Quartermaster Museum, "TIGER—The E-Boat Attack"; Bass, *The Brigades of Neptune*. See also Richard T. Bass. *Exercise Tiger: The D-Day Practice Landing Tragedies Uncovered*. Eastbourne, East Sussex: Tommies Guides, 2008.
25. Report on Operation NEPTUNE. Headquarters, 1st Engineer Special Brigade.
26. Historical Data Report. Headquarters, 519th Port Battalion.
27. Bass, *The Brigades of Neptune*.

CHAPTER 7: THE INVASION

1. Historical Data Report. Headquarters, 519th Port Battalion. According to Peter Sloboda and Herbert Israel, these two port companies had been training in Wales. They were based in Morriston and Mumbles.
2. Ibid.
3. Hopkins, interview by author.
4. Shireman, interview by author.
5. Hopkins, interview by author.
6. Historical Data Report. Headquarters, 519th Port Battalion.
7. Hopkins, interview by author.
8. Balkoski, *Utah Beach*.
9. Hopkins, interview by author.
10. Colby, John. *War from the Ground Up*.
11. Hopkins, interview by author.
12. Ibid.
13. Ibid.
14. Colby, John. *War From The Ground Up*.
15. Ibid. The 90th Infantry Division men were headed to an assembly area near the town of Reuville and would later go on to help the 82nd Airborne rescue an isolated group of their paratroopers on the west side of the Merderet River.

16. Hopkins, interview by author. In 1998 Cortland and the author saw the film *Saving Private Ryan*. While watching the opening sequence, the fight on Omaha Beach, he leaned over and whispered, "That's just how it was."

CHAPTER 8: UTAH BEACH DANGERS

1. Balkoski, *Utah Beach*.

2. Report on Operation NEPTUNE. Headquarters, 1st Engineer Special Brigade.

3. Weaver, interview by author.

4. Shireman, interview by author.

5. Hopkins, interview by author.

6. 304th Port Company Morning Report, June 10, 1944.

7. Sugarman, interview by author; Sonoski, interview by author.

8. Sugarman, interview by author.

9. 304th Port Company Morning Report, June 10, 1944. Killed in action: Lionel L. Ridgeway, Francesco Barone, James E. Curry, Walter M. Slasinski. Wounded in action: Ralph F. Phelen, Dwayne E. Trantham, Raymond D. Hankins. Injured in action: Robert J. Ballenger, Albert J. Karowski, John C. Winfree.

10. Bruce Kramlich provided the author with a document listing port battalion men missing in action. It included three 519th Port Battalion men lost on June 10, 1944: Richard E. Heon, Frank Rodriguez, and George J. Swineheart, Jr. These men were probably all killed in the attack on the SS *Charles Morgan*.

11. Weaver, correspondence with author.

12. Shireman, interview by author.

13. Ibid.

14. Ibid.; Colley, *The Road to Victory*.

15. Hopkins, interview with author.

16. Fullick, "'We performed our mission and did it in a superior manner.'"

17. Shireman, correspondence with author.

18. Ibid.

19. Sugarman, interview by author.

20. Kramlich, correspondence with author.

21. Historical Data Report. Headquarters, 519th Port Battalion.

22. Colley, *The Road to Victory*.

23. Botzon, correspondence with author; Bass, *The Brigades of Neptune*.

24. Hopkins, interview by author.

CHAPTER 9: BEACH WORK

1. Historical Data Report. Headquarters, 519th Port Battalion.

2. Ross, *Destination — Berlin!*, p. 6.

3. Colley, *The Road to Victory*, pp. 40–47.

4. Report on Operation NEPTUNE. Headquarters, 1st Engineer Special Brigade. According to Peter Sloboda, the 280th Port Company landed at Omaha Beach and was trucked overland to Utah Beach.

5. Historical Data Report. Headquarters, 519th Port Battalion.

6. Report on Operation NEPTUNE. Headquarters, 1st Engineer Special Brigade.

7. Historical Data Report. Headquarters, 519th Port Battalion.

8. Ross, *Destination — Berlin!*, p. 6.

9. Report on Operation NEPTUNE. Headquarters, 1st Engineer Special Brigade. "Mulberry" harbors were built on Omaha Beach and Gold Beach. The Mulberry on Omaha Beach was unusable after the June storm.

10. Report on Operation NEPTUNE. Headquarters, 1st Engineer Special Brigade.

11. All the port company men interviewed discussed the unloading process: Fein, Hopkins, Shireman, Sonoski, Sugarman, and Weaver. The ideal unloading situation is detailed in *War Department Training Manual*, No. 55–310.

12. Ibid.

13. Hopkins, interview by author.

14. Weaver, interview by author.

15. Bykofsky and Larson, *United States in World War II*.

16. Hopkins, interview by author.

17. Report on Operation NEPTUNE. Headquarters, 1st Engineer Special Brigade.

18. Colley, *The Road to Victory*, pp. 40–43.

19. Report on Operation NEPTUNE. Headquarters, 1st Engineer Special Brigade; Colley, *The Road to Victory*; Leigh, *American Enterprise in Europe*.

20. Hopkins, interview by author.

21. Shireman, interview by author.

22. Ross, *Destination — Berlin!*

23. Leigh, *American Enterprise in Europe*.

24. Ibid.

25. Colley, *The Road to Victory*.

26. Bykofsky and Larson, *United States in World War II*.

27. Historical Data Report. Headquarters, 519th Port Battalion.

28. Colley, *The Road to Victory.*
29. Bykofsky and Larson, *United States in World War II.*
30. Historical Data Report. Headquarters, 519th Port Battalion; Israel, interview by author.
31. Hopkins, interview by author.
32. Shireman, interview by author.
33. Hopkins, interview by author.
34. Historical Data Report. Headquarters, 519th Port Battalion.
35. "Ack ack" was slang for antiaircraft artillery. "Tracers" are rounds of ammunition that burn brightly to aid the gunners in aiming at night.
36. Sugarman, correspondence with author.

CHAPTER 10: TO ANTWERP

1. Schrijvers, *Liberators.*
2. Zuehlke, *Terrible Victory,* p. 459.
3. Bass, *The Brigades of Neptune,* p. 123.
4. Historical Data Report. Headquarters, 519th Port Battalion; Israel, interview by author.
5. Hopkins, interview by author.
6. Sonoski, interview by author.
7. Hopkins, interview by author.
8. Weaver, correspondence with author.
9. Hopkins, interview by author.
10. For another description of the unusual train ride to Antwerp see Havens, *We Made the Headlines Possible,* p. 59.
11. Historical Data Report. Headquarters, 519th Port Battalion.

CHAPTER 11: THE V-WEAPONS

1. Schrijvers, *Liberators.*
2. Hopkins, interview by author. Tampico Flats is surrounded by four streets: Santiagostraat, Canadalaan, Columbiastraat, and Tampicoplein.
3. Dungan, *V-2*; King and Kutta, *Impact.*
4. Shireman, interview by author.
5. Hopkins, interview by author.
6. Sonoski, interview by author.
7. Hopkins, interview by author.
8. Botzon, correspondence with author.
9. Historical Data Report. Headquarters, 519th Port Battalion.
10. King and Kutta, *Impact,* p. 279.
11. Lockett, "City of Sudden Death."

12. Hopkins, interview by author.
13. Ibid.
14. Shireman, interview by author.
15. King and Kutta, *Impact*, pp. 274 and 279.
16. Document from Headquarters Port Area No. Three, Chanor Base Section Reproduced by HQ 519th Port Bn., July 1945. Provided by Lawrence Botzon.
17. King and Kutta, *Impact*.
18. Ibid.; *The Story of Antwerp X*, p. 39.
19. *184th AAA Gun Bn.*
20. King and Kutta, *Impact*.

CHAPTER 12: WORK IN THE PORT

1. King, "Antwerp," p. 4. King's early draft of his Antwerp chapter in the book *Impact* provides specific boundaries for dock responsibilities: "Allocation of Berths: US Forces to have that portion of the port North of a line drawn through Albert Dock through Berth 140 on the east and between Berths 115 and 117 on the west, including the north portion of Albert Dock, the Leopold Basin, the Vierde Habendock, Quatrieme and the Hansadock adjacent to the Kruisschens Locks. British Forces to have the remainder of the Albert Dock south of this line, and including the Lefebvre Dock and the Amerikadok" (see map p. 114). The author cites the source of this quote as: Historical Section, Office of the Chief of Transportation, European Theater of Operations, *Historical Report of the Transportation Corps in the European Theater of Operations*, Volume V, October-November-December 1944, Part 1, p. 1.
2. King and Kutta, *Impact*, p. 282.
3. Historical Data Report. Headquarters, 519th Port Battalion.
4. Ibid.
5. Colley, *The Road to Victory*, p. 201; King and Kutta, *Impact*, pp. 276–277.
6. For American Railway Grand Divisions in Belgium see Colley, *The Road to Victory*; Gregory, *The Saga of the 708 Railway Grand Division*; King and Kutta, *Impact*; Lockett, "City of Sudden Death." For British/American rail line allocation see: King, "Antwerp."
7. Historical Data Report. Headquarters, 519th Port Battalion.
8. Schrijvers, *Liberators*.
9. King and Kutta, *Impact*.
10. Schrijvers, *Liberators*.
11. Lockett, "City of Sudden Death,"
12. Historical Data Report. Headquarters, 519th Port Battalion; Schrijvers, *Liberators*.
13. Sonoski, interview by author.

14. Schrijvers, *Liberators*.
15. Weaver, interview by author.
16. Schrijvers, *Liberators*.
17. Colley, *The Road to Victory*.
18. Schrijvers, *Liberators*.
19. Weaver, interview by author.
20. Ibid.
21. Bykofsky and Larson, *United States in World War II*, p. 351.
22. Hopkins, interview by author.
23. Weaver, interview by author.
24. Shireman, interview by author.
25. Hopkins, interview by author.
26. Ibid.
27. Ibid.
28. Shireman, interview by author.
29. Ibid.
30. Hopkins, interview by author.
31. Ibid.

CHAPTER 13: THE ARDENNES OFFENSIVE

1. King and Kutta, *Impact*.
2. Sugarman, interview by author.
3. King and Kutta, *Impact*.
4. Hopkins, interview by author.
5. Ibid.

CHAPTER 14: WAR'S END

1. For the effects of the points system see Ambrose, *Band of Brothers*; Schrijvers, *Liberators*.
2. Hopkins, interview by author.
3. Ibid.
4. Ibid.
5. Schrijvers, *Liberators*.
6. *Milwaukee Journal*, Green Sheet.
7. Historical Data Report. Headquarters, 519th Port Battalion.
8. Hopkins, interview by author.
9. Historical Data Report. Headquarters, 519th Port Battalion, April 1945.
10. Historical Data Report. Headquarters, 519th Port Battalion.
11. Ibid.

CHAPTER 15: HOMECOMING

1. Hopkins, interview by author.
2. Ibid.
3. Ibid.
4. Weaver, interview by author.
5. Hopkins, interview by author.
6. Ibid.
7. Ibid.
8. Kramlich, Weaver, and Shireman, interviews by author.
9. Hopkins, interview by author.
10. Hopkins, correspondence to family.

EPILOGUE

1. Hopkins, interview by author.

BIBLIOGRAPHY

OFFICIAL REPORTS AND HISTORIES

Historical Data Report. Headquarters, 519th Port Battalion, APO 228 US Army. 1944–1946.

Company Morning Report, 304th Port Company, 519th Port Battalion, Le Mesnil, Province of Normandy, France. June 10, 1944.

Report on Operation NEPTUNE. Headquarters, 1st Engineer Special Brigade, November 19, 1944.

Bykofsky, Joseph and Larson, Harold. *United States in World War II, The Technical Services, The Transportation Corps: Operations Overseas.* Washington, DC: Center of Military History, 2003.

Leigh, Randolph. *American Enterprise in Europe: The Role of the SOS in the Defeat of Germany.* Paris: Chief Information and Education Division, 1945.

U.S. Army. CIRCULAR No. 228, 1942, Army-Navy Production Award printed in Compilation of War Department General Orders, Bulletins, and Circulars. Washington, DC: US Government Printing Office, 1943.

184th AAA Gun Bn.: Iceland, England, France, Belgium, Holland, Germany. Germany: Printed by Parzeller & Co., bound by Fleischmann of Fulda, 1945.

Nomination for Navy "E" Award by Bureau of Ordinance, April 24, 1942.

War Department Training Manual, Stevedoring and Wharf Handling, No. 55-310. Washington, DC: War Department, May 17, 1943

BOOKLETS

American Locomotive Company. *Growing With Schenectady...* Schenectady, New York, 1948. A history booklet commemorating the 1948 centennial of the company. [Schdy R 621.13 A512] of the Schenectady County Public Library. The text is also available on the web: <http://www.schenectadyhistory.org/railroads/alcohistory>

Rothrock, Gil. *Indianown Gap Military Reservation.* A welcome guide booklet published by Bell Telephone Company of Pennsylvania, 1943.

Ross, Frank. *Destination — Berlin! The Transportation Corps Will Furnish the Necessary Transportation!* Paris: Stars & Stripes / Desfosses-Neogravure, 1944.

The Story of Antwerp X, published by Antwerp X Command, 1945. Scans of this booklet can be found at <http://www.skylighters.org/buzzbombs/antwerpx.html> (accessed viewed on February 7, 2010.)

BOOKS

Ambrose, Stephen E. *Band of Brothers: E Company, 506th Regiment, 101st Airborne from Normandy to Hitler's Eagle's Nest.* 2nd Touchstone ed. New York: Simon & Schuster, 2001.

Balkoski, Joseph. *Utah Beach: The Amphibious Landing and Airborne Operations on D-day, June 6, 1944.* Mechanicsburg, PA: Stackpole Books, 2005.

Bass, Richard T. *The Brigades of Neptune: U.S. Army Engineer Special Brigades in Normandy.* Exeter, Devon: Lee Publishing, 1994.

Gregory, Andrew G. *The Saga of the 708 Railway Grand Division.* Baltimore, MD: Baltimore and Ohio Railroad Comapny, 1947.

Colby, John. *War From The Ground Up: The 90th Division in WWII.* Austin, TX: Nortex Press, 1991.

Colley, David. *The Road to Victory: The Untold Story of World War II's Red Ball Express.* 1st ed. Washington, DC: Brassey's, 2000.

Dungan, Tracy. D. *V-2: A Combat History of the First Ballistic Missile.* Yardley, PA: Westholme Publishing, 2005.

Havens, George N. *We Made the Headlines Possible: The Critical Contribution of the Rear Echelon in World War II.* Cleveland, OH: Greenleaf Book Group, 2003.

Gawne, Jonathan. *Finding Your Father's War: A Practical Guide to Researching and Understanding Service in the World War II US Army.* Philadelphia, PA: Casemate, 2006.

King, Benjamin and Kutta, Timothy. *Impact: The History of Germany's V-Weapons in World War II.* New York: Sarpedon, 1998, pp. 261-286.

Morse, Brian. *A Moment in History: The story of the American Army in Rhondda in 1944.* Talybont, Ceredigion: Y Lofa, 2007

Rottman, Gordon L. *US Combat Engineer 1941–45,* Oxford: Osprey Publishing, 2010.

Rottman, Gordon L. *US World War II Amphibious Tactics: Mediterranean & European Theaters.* Oxford: Osprey Publishing, 2006.

Schrijvers, Peter. *Liberators: The Allies and Belgian Society, 1944–1945.* New York: Cambridge University Press, 2009.

Zuehlke, Mark. *Terrible Victory: First Canadian Army and the Scheldt Estuary Campaign.* Vancouver: Douglas & McIntyre, 2007.

ARTICLES

Belkin, Lisa. "Lucy Monroe Dies: A Celebrated Singer of National Anthem," *New York Times*, October 16, 1987. <http://www.nytimes.com/1987/10/16/obituaries/lucy-monroe-dies-a-celebrated-singer-of-national-anthem.html>

Davis, Grace and Davis, Knickerbacker. "Training Transportation Corps: Port Battalions Load and Unload Ships in Pennsylvania Mountains," *The Philadelphia Inquirer*, August 15, 1943.

Fullick, Brenda. "'We Performed Our Mission and Did It In a Superior Manner': Memories of Another Lifetime, Another World," *The Journal Standard.*

Freeport, IL. June 4, 1994.

King, Benjamin. "Antwerp: Enemy Attack on Supply Lines in Europe 1944-1945,"
p. 4. <http://www.transchool.eustis.army.mil/historian/articles.htm>

Lockett, Edward. "City of Sudden Death," *TIME.* March 26, 1945, pp. 5-6.

Morrison, Allan M. "Port Men Truly Sweat Out Invasion: Army's Stevedores Clear
Masses of Arrving Arms," *The Stars and Stripes*, Vol. 4, No. 170. London.
May 20, 1944.

Noderer, E. R. "Chicagoans on Target Ship of Nazi Bombers," *Chicago Daily
Tribune*, p. 1. June 15, 1944.

Milwaukee Journal, Green Sheet, December 19, 1945.

Schenectady Gazette, "These Honors to Got to Alco Plant, Employees,"
August 11, 1942.

Schenectady Gazette, "Alco and 8,000 Workers Receive 'E' Award Today,"
August 26, 1942.

Schenectady Gazette, "Ingenuity Used at Alco in Building First Tank," American
Locomotive and Schenectady insert, p. 6. August 26, 1942.

Schenectady Gazette, "Alco Given "E" Award as Grim Reminder of Job That Lies
Ahead," August 27, 1942.

Schenectady Gazette, "Alco Here Wins 3 Awards for Production," April 10, 1943.

Schenectady Gazette, "Alco Produced 1st Med. Tank 2 Years Ago: M-3 Was Built in
Five Months from Date of Contract to Award to Co.," April 10, 1943.

Schenectady Gazette, "Churchill, F.D.R. Acclaim 'Desert Victory': Prime Minister
Had Film Flown Here for Showing at White House for President,"
April 10, 1943.

Schenectady Gazette, "General Maxwell Will Address Workers at M-7 Day
Ceremony," April 10, 1943.

Schenectady Gazette, "Howitzer Combined with Tank Chassis: Result Was Weapon
Able to Outshoot, Outrun Any Tanks Germans Had," April 10, 1943.

Schenectady Gazette, "Schenectady Kept Secret of Tank Killer: 'Conspiracy of
Silence' Helped Catch Afrika Korp in Egypt Napping," American Locomotive
and Schenectady insert, p. 16. April 10, 1943.

Schenectady Gazette, "M-7 Praised by British Colonel: Tank Workers Hear Military
Heads, Other Speakers in Saturday's Ceremonies," April 12, 1943.

Wilkin, Jeff. "M-7 Remembered," *The Daily Gazette* (Schenectady, NY).
March 25, 1993.

WEBSITES

Higgs, Delphine. "Delphine's War: Here Come the Yanks." WW2 People's War:
An archive of World War Two memories - written by the public, gathered by
the BBC. <http://www.bbc.co.uk/ww2peopleswar/stories/89/a4073889.shtml>
(accessed June 4, 2009).

Army Quartermaster Museum. "TIGER—The E-Boat Attack: Six Quartermaster
units sustain losses due to enemy action during training for the D-Day
Invasion." Extracted from: Lt. Clifford L. Jones. The Administrative and

Logistical History of the ETP, Part VI: NEPTUNE: Training, Mounting, the Artificial Harbors. Historical Division, United States Army Forces, European Theater. March 1946. <http://www.qmmuseum.lee.army.mil/d-day/tiger.htm> (accessed May 2, 2010).

Penny, John. "The Luftwaffe over Bristol, 1941–1944." Bristol Past: Website of the Fishponds Local History Society. <http://fishponds.org.uk/luftbrim.html> (accessed May 2, 2010).

AUTHOR INTERVIEWS AND CORRESPONDENCE

Bagnato, Dominic L. Interview by author. June 19, 2007.

Botzon, Lawrence. Correspondence with author. December 31, 2009,

Fein, Solomon. Interview by author. February 18, 2010.

Hopkins, Cortland. Interview by author. Multiple days in 2006 (unrecorded); June 12, 19, 20, 22, 28, and 30, 2007; February 2008.

Hopkins, Cortland. Correspondence to family.

Hopkins, Cortland. Interview by Patti Brozyna. June 7, 2009

Israel, Herbert. Interview by author. June 26, and July 5, 2010.

Kramlich, Bruce. Corresponance with author. February, 28, 2007.

Kramlich, Bruce. Interview by author. June 6, December 6, 2009.

Partridge, John. Interview by author. June 30, 2010.
    John Partridge was a young officer in the 13th Major Port. He served in England, Le Havre, and Antwerp.

Shireman, John. Corresponance with author. July 5, 2007.

Shireman, John. Interview by author. June 20, 2007; March 31 and June 6, 2009.

Sloboda, Peter. Interview by author, June 8, 24, and 28, 2010.

Sonoski, Raymond. Interview by author, June, 22, 2007.

Sugarman, Israel. Interview by author. June 6, November 25, and December 3, 2009; Multiple days in 2010.

Weaver, Dave. Interview by author. June 19, 2007; March 31 and June 5, 2009; March 30, 2010.

Weaver, Dave. Corresponance with author. October 16, 2006; March 19 and December 21, 2009.

INDEX

Bruce Kramlich and the author in Colorado, 2009. (AJB)

Dave Weaver and the author in Arizona, 2009. (AJB)

CPSIA information can be obtained at www.ICGtesting.com
Printed in the USA
LVOW011429180911

246799LV00014B/104/P